# Contemporary
# Psychoanalysis
# and
# Religion

# Contemporary Psychoanalysis and Religion

TRANSFERENCE

AND

TRANSCENDENCE

JAMES W. JONES

YALE UNIVERSITY

PRESS

NEW HAVEN

AND LONDON

*Library of Congress Cataloging-in-Publication Data*

Jones, James William.
Contemporary psychoanalysis and religion : transference and
transcendence / James W. Jones.
p.    cm.
Includes bibliographical references and index.
ISBN: 978-0-300-05784-3 (paper)

1. Psychoanalysis and religion. 2. Transference (Psychology)
3. Transcendence (Philosophy) I. Title.
BF175.4.R44J65   1991
200'.1'9—dc20           90-41776

A catalogue record for this book is available
from the British Library.

Printed in the United States of America

To Elizabeth

# CONTENTS

Preface

ix

Introduction

A NEW PSYCHOANALYSIS
AND THE STUDY OF RELIGION

1

Chapter 1

MODELS OF RELATIONSHIP

9

Chapter 2

TRANSFERENCE AND TRANSCENDENCE

34

Chapter 3

TRANSFERENCE AND THE
DYNAMICS OF RELIGION

68

Chapter 4

TRANSFERENCE AND TRANSFORMATION

86

Chapter 5

TOWARD A PSYCHOANALYSIS
OF THE SACRED

111

# CONTENTS

**References**
137

**Index**
143

# PREFACE

Most days I shuttle between two fields. Geography is a metaphor for my life. I spend part of my day in a classroom trying to interest students in the wisdom of the Buddha or the sayings of Jesus and how they might be interpreted philosophically or understood against the backdrop of modern physics or psychology. And I spend a part of my evenings in an office where I listen to depressed and suicidal businessmen or couples on the edge of divorce.

This book attempts to work in the space between the disciplines of religious studies and clinical psychology. It is written by someone who has studied, taught, and written about the forms that religion has taken in humanity's history and some of the categories used to understand them, earning a doctorate in religious studies, and who has also been trained in the investigation of human behavior and the relief of aspects of human suffering, earning another doctorate in clinical psychology.

Thus this is a very personal book, growing out of many years of occupying the space between these fields. To my colleagues in religious studies, I hope to offer a new perspective on a subject they already know well. To my colleagues in psychology, especially psychodynamic psychology, I hope to provide a fresh treatment of a pervasive human experience.

Several people have contributed to this project. I am grateful to the members of an ongoing seminar on object relations theory and the study of religion who first aroused my interest in this topic. Behind this seminar is the inspiration of Bill and Marilyn Saur who, through countless discussions, stimulated much of the thinking that went into this book. Mal Diamond and John McDargh have been afflicted with earlier versions, and their comments and criticisms have immeasurably strengthened the present one. Charles Grench of Yale University Press provided encouragement when it was most needed, and the suggestions of his anonymous reviewers added considerably to its final form. The psycho-analytic framework utilized in the coming pages suggests that the themes of one's writing often mirror the themes of one's life; the central theme of this book is the relational self and in that regard Elizabeth Burk has added more to my life than any writing can express.

# Contemporary
# Psychoanalysis
# and
# Religion

# INTRODUCTION

## A NEW PSYCHOANALYSIS AND THE STUDY OF RELIGION

Since the inception of the psychoanalytic study of religion, Freudian and Jungian paradigms have dominated it. The term *analysis* comes from the Greek word meaning to loosen; just as descendants of Isaac Newton and Robert Boyle were "loosening" the structure of matter, breaking it down into atoms and molecules, so Sigmund Freud's goal was to break down the patterns of human behavior into their component energies and mechanisms. To understand meant to analyze, to lay bare the structures beneath the surface. And Freud possessed the heuristic courage to follow the analytic trail however deep it led into the caverns of the mind.

An heir of the Enlightenment, Freud assumed that atheism was normative and religion was but a vestige of the childhood of humankind. Psychoanalysis was to complete the Comptian project of the vanquishing of religion by science, extending the hegemony of Newtonian mechanism and Darwinian naturalism into the depths of the soul. The sublimest ecstasies and the most profound sensibilities were to be broken down into their instinctual components and the mechanics of lust and aggression.

In the course of his life, Freud offered several accounts of the origin of religion. In *Totem and Taboo*, he diagnosed religion as an "obsessional neurosis," an attempt to ward off guilt by repetition. The guilt arises, he

1

said, from the unconscious murderous wishes of the son desiring to kill the father. Freud claimed that this desire was acted out in history when the sons of the first tribe arose and killed their patriarch and then, out of guilt, idealized the dead father and enshrined him as their god. Thus the origin of religion lies in the oedipal struggle that is reenacted in the life of every boy, laying down the psychological foundation for religion: guilt at the oedipal wishes, which is assuaged through the obsessive repetition of ritual and reconciliation to an idealized patriarchal father god. By rooting religion in the instinctual life of the child, Freud offered a biological hermeneutic of the sacred.

In *The Future of an Illusion*, Freud suggested that, through fantasy, religion reduces the terror of an uncaring nature by personalizing the natural order, removes the fear of death by providing an illusion of immortality, and reconciles us to the social necessity of self-denial by promising to reward us for it in the hereafter. Freud was confident that the future would bring a weakening of the religious illusion. Infantile needs for protection, comfort, compensation, and the assuaging of guilt are common in the world of the child, but they are destined to be outgrown.

A son of Abraham, Freud could neither shake free of the heritage of Torah nor submit to it. On the one hand, moral responsibility, especially to the demands of truth, is the pinnacle of human maturity; on the other hand, conscience in the form of the superego is but the residue of the boy's oedipal desire to kill his father and ravish his mother combined with the social necessity of instinctual restraint.

Furthermore, like all machines, the psyche requires energy, and its libidinal force should not be squandered in fantasy but rather stored and channeled—"sublimated," in Freud's term—into the higher mental functions of science and logic. Thus control of the passions was as important to Freud as it was to any Platonic or Puritan ascetic. Only control can make the basic energy available for productive work, but overcontrol builds up too much instinctual energy, which can then come out only as a neurotic symptom. Freud's solution was, in the words of his basic maxim, "where id is, let ego be"—where instincts exist, let rational self-control rather than irrational repression reign. Taking responsibility for oneself and voluntarily choosing the path of self-control, then, became the core of his moral code (Rieff 1959; Van Herik 1982).

Thus Freud's ambivalence about religion. He wrote in *The Future of an Illusion*, "If [religion] succeeded in making the majority of mankind happy, in comforting them, in reconciling them to life, and in making them into vehicles of civilization, no one would dream of attempting to alter the existing conditions" ([1927] 1964:61). To the extent that religion performed a civilizing function and kept instinctual chaos at bay, Freud could approve of it. But, of course, Freud was living at a time when religion appeared to be losing its grip on the hearts and minds of men and women, and his own work could only accelerate that trend. If society was to be kept from lapsing into instinctual chaos, religion could not simply be destroyed; it had to be replaced. Thus the maxim of the ego being where the id is was not only a prescription for mental health; it was also a harbinger of a cultural revolution in which knowledge would be governed by reason rather than by superstition, and morality by self-control rather than by ecclesiastical authority. (Further discussion of Freud's impact on modern culture can be found in Rieff 1959.)

Psychoanalysis, by providing what Freud termed an "education to reality" ([1927] 1964:81), would render religion implausible and unnecessary. Seen as the projection of infantile wishes, religion would lose any semblance of credibility. Taught the rational importance of self-control, civilized people would no longer require pious authoritarianism. Health would require renouncing the wondrous but unattainable wishes of childhood for the realistic but prosaic satisfactions of adulthood. Thus illusions of comfort, protection, and compensation should be put aside and responsibilities shouldered; piety should be relinquished, and morality assumed.

If Freud sought the renunciation and sublimation of religion into science and morality, Carl Jung (1938) sought its transformation into a universal form of wisdom. Jung, as is well known, never fully accepted Freud's libido theory and the Darwinian reduction of behavior to instinct. Rather he asserted the autonomy of the psyche, cutting it loose from soma. For example, in working with dreams, Freud decoded the dream imagery in terms of instinctual wishes, applying to the dream the reduction of psychological phenomena to biological states. For Jung, in contrast, each dream had a psychic integrity of its own that was not to be collapsed into a system of libidinous levers and pulleys. Trying to remain for a time within his master's orbit, Jung spoke of libido, but it was not Freud's pleasure-seeking instinct. Rather it was an undifferentiated psychic energy that could be expressed in a variety of equally valid forms and images.

Examining Jung's dream interpretations, Freud quickly realized that his disciple had departed from him in a radical way. Their differences over the definition of libido were more than simply semantic. If libido was not primarily sexual, then the drive to find the physiological basis for psychological events that promised to make psychoanalysis into a respectable science, the edifice of the oedipal complex on which the entire theory of neurosis depended, the reductionistic program that drove Freud's tireless appetite for work—all would and did collapse. Jung abandoned the biological hermeneutic of the psyche: he made no attempt at a physiological psychology, he made little use of the oedipal drama, and his thinking was rarely reductionistic.

Neurosis arises, said Jung, not from repressed instincts but from split-off parts of the self that he called "complexes"—parts split off and repressed because they do not fit with our image of ourselves or the persona that our culture reinforces. Thus a man who considers himself totally rational will split off and repress his emotional side or a woman who sees herself as dependent will hide her strengths from herself and others. And since the psyche is androgynous, all men contain a feminine aspect (called the "anima") which they tend to repress, whereas women tend to silence their masculine side (called the "animus"). But for Jung the fundamental psychological drive is not gratification but integration, and so the psyche struggles to become conscious of and draw upon these hidden but real dimensions of the self, a process Jung called "individuation." The task of analysis is to facilitate this process.

Encyclopedic in his breadth of knowledge, Jung began to notice that many of the images carrying the major themes of individuation that occurred in his patients' dreams echoed images from other cultures and other times: for example, in many cultures water is a symbol for rebirth, and the mandala (the superimposition of square and circle) is a sign of wholeness and personal integration. Others had noticed this, but Jung considered it more than coincidence; these were data worthy of investigation. From his cross-cultural examination of symbolism, Jung concluded that personal consciousness is but a superficial layer of material floating atop a virtually infinite sea of shared images and themes that he called "archetypes." This collection of archetypical material he first termed the "collective unconscious" to emphasize its universality and later called the "objective psyche" to stress its transcendence of the individual conscious ego. Thus individuation came to involve the recovery not simply of suppressed parts of our personality but also of the universal aspects of human nature.

Religion, Jung said, is the traditional shepherd of the process of individuation. Its symbols and rituals resonate to those repressed but significant aspects of the unconscious, both individual and collective. Religion had served in the past to keep men and women open to their depths. But with the decline of religion in a modern, secular society, people had lost touch with the most universal concerns of humankind and the healing powers of the archetypical psyche. Thus the task of Jungian analysis was not just the cure of personal neurosis but also the recovery of the sacred buried within each self. In pursuit of this goal, Jung's psychology became a theology in disguise—envisioning a universal power outside of conscious control that brings health and wholeness when accessed through dream, symbol, and intuitive experience (Homans 1979).

Jung's psychotheology speaks on one hand of *archetypical* themes and a *collective* unconscious, thus appearing to bind humankind together. On the other hand, Jungian theory, like its creator, is profoundly introverted and individualistic—each person his or her own church, synagogue, or ashram. One has no need of others; everyone has within the self the collective wisdom of the human race. (This impression is reinforced by reading Jung's autobiography, *Memories, Dreams and Reflections* [1961], in which a man who lived through many of the climactic events of the early twentieth century hardly makes reference to the happenings he witnessed that shook Europe and Western civilization to its core.) Jungian analysis begins and ends with the individual, perhaps under the direction of a wise analytic guide, alone with his or her memories and dreams and images.

Freud's antipathy toward the collective and his exaltation of the autonomous individual come through clearly on every page of *Totem and*

*Taboo* and are expressed in even more extreme form in his later works, *Group Psychology and the Analysis of the Ego* and *Civilization and Its Discontents*. They portray only chronic conflict between the individual, driven by a pleasure-seeking id, and the inevitable demands of group and social membership. His intrapsychic theory of psychopathology in which neurosis arises from the inherent conflict of instincts detaches the individual and his or her suffering from any particular interpersonal context. Culture enters into Freud's model and into the typography of character under the rubric of the superego, an aspect of the personality that is destined to grow weaker over time as the rational ego gains hegemony over the blind id and the moralistic conscience (Rieff 1959).

Most psychoanalytic investigation of religion has taken place in either a Freudian or a Jungian context. These paradigms have been, and remain, extremely fruitful in the psychology of religion, as attested by the steady stream of papers and books that continues to come from their respective researchers. But these two psychological frameworks are only the background to the present study. It is the contention of this book that newer post-Freudian and post-Jungian models of psychoanalytic understanding have much to contribute to the psychological investigation of religion.

Unlike both Freud and his erstwhile son Jung, contemporary approaches to the dynamics of personality begin with interpersonal experience rather than with the individual as a heuristically self-contained system of instinctual or archetypal forces. Personality and psychopathology are derived from the vicissitudes of interaction rather than from conflicts generated by repressed biological or spiritual energies. (These developments are reviewed in Greenberg and Mitchell 1983.) Such models shift the focus of psychoanalytic understanding from the isolated individual to the process of interaction, viewing the self as constellated from internalized interpersonal episodes. These internalized patterns of interaction and not biological drives or universal themes are expressed in our everyday behavior, including our religion or its absence.

Nowhere is this shift in focus clearer than in theories about the nature of the relationship between the analyst and the patient. Freud described the analytic relationship by using the term *transference:* patients were understood to be transferring onto the analyst their instinctually based childhood wishes, fears, and behaviors. Freud understood religion, too, as a form of transference in which the same defense mechanism of projection was at work. In both the analytic setting and the practices of piety, the patient or devotee was projecting childhood conflicts onto a blank screen. In continuity with Freud, the idea of the transference will be the lens through which religion will be examined in this study, too.

But the current shift in psychoanalytic theorizing toward a focus on interactional patterns has profound implications for the study of religion. The application of such models casts new light on its psychological aspects, bringing into the open aspects of religion overlooked in the paradigms of Freud and Jung. Others have begun applying these newer psychoanalytic theories to religion (McDargh 1983; Pruyser 1968; Rizzuto 1979), but none has used the transference (as Freud did) as the central category for researching and understanding religion.

The first chapter of this book sketches in detail the newer models of transference. The second suggests some implications for investigating religion and some of the themes that might emerge from psychoanalytic research into the connection of transference phenomena and religious experience; it also contrasts this approach with other recent psychoanalytic studies of religion. The third chapter begins such an investigation by discussing four cases, drawing parallels between the dynamics operative in the individuals' transferences and their religious experiences before and during therapy. The fourth chapter draws on two models of psychotherapeutic change—those of developmental object relations theory and self psychology illustrated by Masterson and Kohut—to understand the transformations that took place psychologically and religiously in these four people in the course of treatment.

Whereas chapters 3 and 4 begin with the psychologies of the people and point to connections between their dynamics and their religious experiences, the fifth chapter begins from the other end of the argument. It starts with the experience of the sacred rather than with intrapsychic patterns. One of the major methodological conflicts between religious studies and psychoanalysis as they have developed in the twentieth century involves precisely this issue: a rejuvenation of theology in the West took place in midcentury around the assertion that reflection on religion must begin with God rather than with human experience as had been the case in the mainstream of nineteenth-century European theology; in contrast, psychoanalysis continued Freud's trajectory of reducing religious concepts to intrapsychic dynamics (Homans 1970). Chapter 5, the last, will suggest that current models of psychoanalytic investigation may provide a way past this dichotomy, illustrating this suggestion with a dialogue involving selected psychoanalysts and theologians.

# CHAPTER

# 1

## MODELS OF
## RELATIONSHIP

The book begins, in these first two chapters, with a broad theoretical perspective, outlining the history of Freudian and post-Freudian psychoanalytic theories of transference and something of their possible application to the study of religion. The scope of these developments will be traced, along with the emergence of a new model of human nature which they represent.

### *Freud and Traditional Psychoanalysis*

In the beginning of psychoanalysis, Josef Breuer and Sigmund Freud spoke of the patient transferring "onto the figure of the physician the distressing ideas which arise from the content of the analysis" (1893–1895:302). At the end of his career, in *An Outline of Psychoanalysis,* Freud wrote of the transference in such phrases as "the patient sees in his analyst the return—the reincarnation—of some important figure out of his childhood or past, and consequently transfers onto him feelings and reactions that undoubtedly applied to this model," and so "again and again what he [the patient] takes to be new real life is a reflection of the past" ([1940] 1948:68, 69).

Freud's model of the transference contains two elements. First, the idea of repetition: for Freud, the tyranny of the past is supreme. Present-day encounters invariably follow in tracks established in the child's first interactions.

> The individual's emotional attitudes to other people . . . are already established at an unexpectedly early age. . . . [They] have already been laid down in the first six years of his life. . . . All those whom he gets to know later become substitute figures for these first objects. . . . All of his later choices of friendship and love follow upon the basis of the memory-traces left behind by these prototypes. (1914:243)

Our earliest relationships, then, form a template into which all later interactions fit. The present resembles the past partly because we choose to relate to people who naturally fit the mold of our parents and partly because we work hard to force them to fit it when they do not do so naturally.

Nowhere is this truer than in the relationship of patient and analyst. Given the neutrality of the analyst, it is easy for the patient to interact with him or her in the old way. Thus the analysis of the transference becomes the centerpiece of treatment, for in the transference the patient's neurotic feelings, wishes, and desires stand out clearly. Since the meaning of all present-day actions lies in their replaying of the past, transference interpretations are backward facing, uncovering the childhood roots of current relationships.

The second element in Freud's understanding of the transference is his idea of the primacy of instinct. The basic motivation for human behavior is biological drive. Psychopathology results from the person's repressing these instincts and the fantasies and wishes they generate, rendering them unconscious and then engaging in defensive maneuvers—denying feelings, projecting them onto others, keeping an overly tight rein on them—to keep them unconscious. Neurotic behavior arises from these defensive activities and the repressed instinctual energy seeking a channel of expression.

Again, this is true particularly in the transference which, for Freud, is a form of neurosis whose patterns represent the reenacting of these instinctually based wishes and drives ([1940] 1948:69). Given the conflict between instincts (especially eros and thanatos, as described in *Beyond the Pleasure Principle*) and the defenses against them, every behavior represents a trade-off between opposing forces. The conflict between instincts becomes the ambivalence that dogs all our activities. This too shows up clearly in the analytic relationship: "This transference is ambivalent: it compromises positive and affectionate as well as negative and hostile attitudes toward the analyst, who, as a rule, is put in the place of one or another of the patient's parents" ([1940] 1948:66).

These two elements are connected by Freud's biologically grounded assumption that instinctual needs, being inherent in the organism, continually drive for satisfaction and release. Thus another reason the transference repeats the past, besides the power of the prototypical childhood, is that instinctually driven patterns are bound to recur. Transference is just one example of the inevitable repetition of instinctually motivated behaviors.

Freud's model of transference as instinctually driven repetition has continued, and been strengthened, in the ensuing development of psychoanalysis. Almost thirty years after *An Outline of Psychoanalysis,* Greenson, in his textbook of psychoanalytic technique, defines transference in words Freud could have written:

> The main characteristic [of the transference] is the experience of feelings to a person which do not befit that person and which actually apply to another. Essentially a person in the present is reacted to as though he were a person in the past. Transference is a repetition, a new edition of an old object relationship. A displacement has taken place; impulses, feelings, and defenses pertaining to a person in the past have been shifted onto a person in the present. (1967:152)

Greenson affirms that transference is a "distortion" that is "always inappropriate."

For contemporary analysts like Greenson, as well as Greenacre (1954), Eissler (1958), Fenichel (1941), and others, the transference is the centerpiece of treatment. In Greenson's words, "psychoanalysis is distinguished from all other therapies by the way it promotes the development of the transference reactions and how it attempts systematically to analyze transference material" (1967:151).

Like Freud, these analysts stress the instinctual basis of the transference. The fantasies, wishes, and impulses that find expression in the transference remain rooted in the "instinctual frustration and the search for gratification [that] are the basic motives for transference phenomena" (Greenson 1967:177). Fenichel's imagery, taken from Freud, represents the fluid dynamics of the psyche, describing how transference results from impulses that are "blocked," "dammed-up," or flowing in "distorted channels," until they are finally discharged at the analyst (1941, chap. 2).

For these analysts, transference represents a regression to infantile thoughts and feelings. Thus it is inevitably inappropriate (Greenson 1967:155), injecting the past where it does not belong, in the present. Thus transference experiences represent a break, if not a breakdown, of ego functioning and reality testing in the present (Fenichel 1941; Greenson 1967; Racker 1954).

In some ways these more recent theoreticians outdo Freud in their concern that the analyst remain totally neutral and respect rather than interfere with the transference. The analyst must remain completely detached and incognito. For example, Greenacre (1954) implies that analysts should refrain from even appearing in public and should not be associated with any social-political causes or act as public figures in any way—a stricture Freud himself hardly followed. Any attempt to (as they phrase it) "manipulate the transference" and "gratify the patient" by words of advice, encouragement, sympathy, or support destroys the objectivity of analysis and threatens the patient and the treatment. (This point is argued at length in Greenson 1967, Greenacre 1954, Fenichel 1941, Racker 1954.) This manipulation of the transference accounts for the illusion of help provided by nonanalytic therapies. Greenson suggests that all "deviant" approaches to psychotherapy "can be described by some aberration in the way the transference situation is handled" (1967:151). And Fenichel (1941) and others disparage all nonanalytic treatment as providing only "transference cures" in which patients appear to improve because of the support and advice of the therapist but are not really "cured" for they have not come to terms with deeper, instinctual material. When Eissler (1958) suggests that sometimes "variations in psychoanalytical technique" may be necessary, he stresses that such "parameters" are to be introduced with the utmost caution and withdrawn as soon as possible. This concern to "safeguard the transference" (Greenson's phrase, 1967:271) becomes the hallmark of Freudian psychoanalysis.

This emphasis is consistent with a model of psychopathology arising from unconscious instinctual forces seeking to become conscious. Within this framework, lasting cure demands making conscious these repressed fantasies and wishes and so they must be allowed undisturbed expression in a neutral milieu—that is, the transference. Given the logical connection between the traditional psychoanalytic understanding of the transference and the entire body of Freudian theory, especially the primacy of instincts and oedipal desires, any thorough attempt to rethink the nature of the transference could take place only as part of a more general rethinking of psychoanalytic theory. For example, in the 1940s Franz Alexander suggested that the transference should be regarded as a "corrective emotional experience," in which patients undergo and learn from experiences of warmth and understanding (presumably lacking in their early years) and thereby become healed (Alexander 1963). This suggestion was rejected out of hand by analysts as an attempt to manipulate rather than analyze the transference (see, for example, Greenson 1967:170). Part of the problem with Alexander's proposal was that he attempted to insert an alien notion into the larger body of psychoanalytic theorizing without reworking other, interconnected, aspects of the theory. Conversely, any revisions of psychoanalytic theories of personality and psychopathology would eventually have an impact on the understanding of the transference.

## W. R. D. Fairbairn

One of the fundamental revisions of psychoanalytic theory was carried out by the British school of object relations theorists, of which the work of W. R. D. Fairbairn will, for our purposes, be taken as representative. While torturing the language in an attempt to maintain continuity with Freud, Fairbairn in one brief sentence breaks decisively with the biologism of his predecessor: "Libidinal aims are of secondary importance in comparison with object-relations. . . . a relationship with an object and not the gratification of an impulse is the ultimate aim of libidinal striving" (1943:50). In Freud's biologically driven theory, the primary motivation is simply the release of pent-up tension. The object of that impulse is of lesser importance. For Fairbairn it is precisely the object and an entering into relationship with that object that is the primary human motivation. In classical Freudian terms, there is no transition from narcissistic to object libido; we are object seeking, relationally oriented, from the beginning.

Theories of motivation are closely tied with models of personality. Our primary motivation is to establish object relations, says Fairbairn, and our personality is structured around the internalization of these relations. These relationships provide the primary data of psychoanalytic inquiry, for "psychology may be said to resolve itself into a study of the relationships of the individual to his objects" (1943:60). Understanding personality means understanding the processes by which external object relations become the internal structures of personality. Understanding a person means grasping the world of his or her inner object relations.

It is a peculiarity of Fairbairn's theory that the process of internalization—the process that constellates human personality—is primarily a defense. Because the objects of our experience are painful, we are "compelled to internalize them in an effort to control them" (1943:67). But it doesn't work. The defense turns out to be a Trojan horse. By taking these bad objects inside us, they remain with us seemingly forever, and they "retain their power . . . in the inner world" (1943:67). There they live on as "internal saboteurs"—the conflicting camp of anxious, guilty, condemning inner voices. Thus personality appears to be at its root a defense against pain, with a core of psychopathology in every personality. For "it is impossible for anyone to pass through childhood without having bad objects which are internalized and repressed" (1943:64). Thus just as psychology is the study of object relations, "psychopathology may be said to resolve itself more specifically into a study of the relationships of ego to its internalized objects" (1943:60).

Bad objects—that is to say rejecting, persecuting, unresponsive parents and caretakers—are internalized. But since they are as painful in the inner world as they were in the outer, they are often repressed as well as internalized. Object relations, then, provide the key to repression as well as to motivation and personality, for "what are primarily repressed are neither intolerably guilty impulses nor intolerably unpleasant memories, but intolerably bad internalized objects" (1943:62).

The parent's behavior in relation to the child is the root of the processes of internalization and repression, and so it is important to note that what is really internalized is the affective relationship or the emotional tone of the parent-child bond rather than the parent as a static thing or object. Although Fairbairn's language is ambiguous on this important point, the thrust of his argument clearly is that what is internalized is an object *relation*. But by continually using Melanie Klein's phrase "internalized objects," he often gives the impression that we take into ourselves static objects.

Unfortunately, repression does not rid us of the bad objects we have taken in. They are out of sight but not out of mind. In an attempt to rid ourselves of them, we project them onto the external world in a process Fairbairn calls "projective identification," another term borrowed from Melanie Klein. The inner world is then, once again, played out in the external one. Someone is scripted into the role of, say, unavailable father, and another, perhaps, gets to play the part of the overinvolved mother. The same holds true for a rejecting parent, an abandoning parent, or a critical one. First they are internalized and repressed and then—unconsciously, to be sure—projected back onto the external world.

Again, it is crucial to remember that what is re-created in this process of projective identification is not simply a bad object (one more controlling mother or critical father) but more significantly, a bad object relationship. Once again the individual can fight against a controlling father, be humiliated by a critical mother, pursue a distant parent, or be the favored child of a doting grandmother.

The implications for understanding the transference are obvious. The same projective mechanisms are at work with the analyst. But here too, the goal is not the discharge of libido and aggression (as Freud thought) but the re-creation of an object relationship. In the transference, the bad objects are projected onto the analyst. As with Freud, the transference is both the problem and the solution to the problem. It is the problem in that the neurosis is played out in the transference and the analyst is asked to carry the various bad object projections. It is the solution in that the process is thus made conscious and is available for interpretation.

For Fairbairn, as for Freud, the transference is a repetition, and the mechanism of projective identification explains why this is so: not because instinctual pleasure always seeks to be experienced again and again but because we find or create carriers for the same bad object projections over and over again.

In terms of theory, Fairbairn makes radical departures from Freud. In terms of technique he continues the assertion that the analyst is a neutral screen for the patient's projections and that the unconscious (bad objects) is made conscious through interpretation. The one difference, and it is crucial, is that the interpretation of the transference focuses not on repressed instincts but on the replaying of bad object relationships. Thus feelings of guilt, "badness," anxiety, and so on "should be related by interpretation to bad object situations" (1943:74). One feels bad, guilty, or anxious not because of unacceptable impulses but because one has internalized a bad, guilt-provoking, or anxious object.

Fairbairn, like Freud, seems persuaded that making the unconscious conscious is enough to cure the problem and, in this case, "dissolve the attachment to the bad object." The transference, then, is necessary but ancillary to the treatment; it is not itself a cause or cure. The sufficiency of consciousness for cure, however, makes sense only in the context of Freud's instinct theory in which the problem is the repression of the instincts pure and simple. For Freud, troubled interpersonal relationships are the result of repression. For Fairbairn it is the reverse. Repression results from bad object relationships. Because the object relationship is painful, it causes the process of repression to be employed.

If the problem is not simply repression but badly constituted relationships, then consciousness alone may not be sufficient for cure. Badly constituted relationships must be replaced by more gracious ones. Thus the transference would be not simply an aid to the treatment but would itself become the main vehicle for treatment. Although consistent with his theory, that was a step Fairbairn seemed unwilling to take.

### Heinz Kohut

It was a step that Heinz Kohut was willing to make, however, moving beyond Fairbairn in consistently applying an object relations perspective not only to understanding personality and psychopathology but to therapy as well.

We are born in relation; we live and die there. As Kohut says simply, "A self can never exist outside a matrix of selfobjects" (1984:61). By self-objects Kohut means those relationships through which we "maintain the cohesion, vitality, strength, and harmony of the self" (1984:197). Just as, when referring to objects, Fairbairn is really referring to relationships, Kohut, too, when speaking of selfobjects, is really speaking of a particular kind of relationship—the kind that is necessary for a strong sense of self. Not traumatic events but "the history of the parents' whole relationship with the child" (1971:80) contains the seeds of later problems. And, more specifically, it is the affective tone of the selfobject relationship that is most significant, for "the child experiences the feeling states of the selfobject . . . as if they were his own" (1977:86).

But Fairbairn's language—"internalized objects"—often betrays this insight because for Fairbairn, internalization is virtually a process of swallowing the object whole where it lives on inside the personality, a psychologically miniature version of its anxious, critical, or angry external self. The self is virtually a reflection of its object relations. On the other hand, Kohut seems more consistent in maintaining that what is internalized are *patterns of relatedness:* "the basic units [of the self] are . . . the complex experiences and action patterns of a self/selfobject unit" (1977:49). And rather than their being simply taken in, Kohut stresses that selfobject experiences are "transmuted" or transformed into the "psychic structures" that make us who we are, that is, our goals, ambitions, values, our capacities for care and commitment (1971:49).

The importance of object relations is not simply developmental. For Fairbairn, it seems, we are dependent on object relations in childhood for our personality development, but, as with Freud, as we mature, we become increasingly independent. Not so for Kohut. In one sentence he rejects the progression latent in all modern psychological theories of development, writing that "a move from dependency (symbiosis) to independence (autonomy) is an impossibility and that the developmental moves of normal psychological life must be seen in the changing nature of the relationships between the self and its selfobjects" (1984:52). Even at our psychologically most developed, we can never move beyond the perimeter of selfobject relations.

The priority given to relationships elevates the transference to central importance. According to Kohut there are three fundamental relational needs (he calls them selfobject transferences) necessary to develop a solid sense of self: the idealizing transference, or the need to be connected to a greater, ideal reality; the mirroring transference, or the need for recognition and acceptance; and the twinship transference, or the need to experience that others are like us. These three experiences are the foundations of our ambitions, our goals, and our use of our skills and talents, respectively. These three needs—"his need to experience mirroring and acceptance; his need to experience merger with greatness, strength, and calmness; and his need to experience the presence of essential alikeness"—are never outgrown but remain throughout our lives, existing "from the moment of birth to the moment of death" (1984:194, punctuation slightly altered).

For Freud, transference is something to be outgrown. For Kohut we never outgrow transference, only move from childish to adult forms. The human needs for dependency, connection, affirmation, even symbiosis, are never left behind, just transformed into more mature forms. Transference is the result not of the drive of biological instincts to seek release and relief but rather of the inherent human condition of relatedness and the drive for those empathic resonances that sustain us as human beings. Human life cannot exist in "the absence of that responsive selfobject milieu" (1984:21).

Thus differences between Freud and Kohut can be understood developmentally, by a kind of historical empathy, in terms of the dialectics of cultural evolution. Freud and modernity typify the necessary discovery of individuality and autonomy after the medieval symbiosis; Kohut represents the postmodern need to rediscover connection and communion in a way that does not undermine autonomy and individuality but continues a genuine evolution beyond both the enmeshments of medieval society and the brittle autonomies of modernity. Freud's theories then can be understood as phase-appropriate but not absolute. (Background on this model of cultural development can be found in Jones 1982, 1977.)

So the distinction between self and selfobjects is important only heuristically. In real life the self and its relationships are one. The main priority for the self is developing and maintaining a cohesive sense of itself. Kohut writes, "it is the self and the survival of its nuclear program that is the basic force in everyone's personality" (1984:147) and "the struggles of the self and its attempt to safeguard its potentials have clear priority" (1984:148). But Kohut makes it clear that these phrases are not to be interpreted solipsistically. He is talking not about the isolated self but about a self that can exist only in relationship. Selfobject relations are the only means for the preservation of a core sense of selfhood. To repeat Kohut's basic maxim: "a self can never exist outside a matrix of selfobjects." All the activities of the psyche—its actions, relationships, jobs, art and music, philosophies and religions—are to be understood not as defenses against the instincts (Freud) nor as ways of creating meaning (as suggested by Atwood, Stolorow, and Lachmann who will be discussed shortly) but rather as ways of maintaining a cohesive sense of self through mirroring and idealizing connections with necessary selfobjects.

Maturity, then, consists not in the outgrowing of relationships but in the capacity to form satisfying and self-sustaining ones, to pick appropriate rather than frustrating and depriving objects for our emotional investment and to be open and vulnerable enough to allow them to nourish us.

> The essence of the psychoanalytic cure resides in the patient's newly acquired ability to identify and seek out appropriate selfobjects—both mirroring and idealizable—as they present themselves in his realistic surroundings and to be sustained by them. . . . it increases the self's ability to use selfobjects for its own sustenance, including an increased freedom in choosing selfobjects. (1984:77)

Kohut cites several examples of mature selfobject relations: an increased capacity to be reassured by a friend's wordlessly putting his arm around one's shoulder, the ability to feel strengthened and uplifted when listening to music, the ability to exhibit joyfully the products of one's creativity in order to obtain the approval of a responsive selfobject audience (1984:76).

For Freud, the needs of the child are always unrealistic and can never be met but must be renounced. For Kohut, the needs of the child must first be met and then gradually frustrated (by a process he calls "transmuting internalization") so that selfobjects can be internalized as self structures. Of course, they are speaking of very different kinds of childhood needs. Freud's, being instinctual, must be renounced—killing one parent and possessing the other is unrealistic, whereas Kohut's, being narcissistic, are not. It is not too much to expect some mirroring, empathy, idealizability, and twinship.

Those dichotomies between autonomy and dependency, individualism and collectivism, that have poisoned the modern age are false, Kohut suggests. There is really no contradiction between individuality and belonging. Actually belonging to a matrix of selfobjects is necessary for that cohesive sense of self that is the precondition for individuality. In an empathic selfobject matrix there is belonging and connection along with individuality and autonomy—one cannot exist without the other. We are interconnected, part of a larger matrix. Kohut is talking here about the same reality as general systems theory but in a very different language. We exist only as a part of a system, a system of selfobjects.

The primacy of selfobject relationships also governs Kohut's discussion of psychopathology and psychotherapy. For Freud, psychopathology arises from wholly intrapsychic factors: the conflict between basic instinctual drives and the demands of social and moral reality represented intrapsychically as the ego and superego. For Fairbairn and Kohut, it is painful interpersonal relations rather than conflicted intrapsychic structures that are at the root of later problems. In a sweeping statement, Kohut asserts that "all forms of psychopathology . . . . are due to disturbances of selfobject relationships in childhood" (1984:53). For Fairbairn, however, pathology results because these bitter interactions must be taken into the psychic (in the vain hope of mastering them) from whence they continue to sabotage the individual. For Kohut, it is precisely the reverse. Because they are so bitter, these object relations cannot be internalized and therefore the individual fails to develop a strong and cohesive sense of self. If optimal internalization does not take place,

> the child does not acquire the needed internal structure, his psyche remains fixated on an archaic selfobject, and the personality will throughout life be dependent on certain objects in what seems to be an intense form of object

hunger. The intensity of the search for and dependency on these objects is due to the fact that they are striven for as a substitute for the missing segments of the psychic structure. (1971:45)

Fairbairn and Kohut appear to be addressing rather different forms of psychopathology, perhaps the difference contained in the traditional distinction between neurosis and character disorders. Fairbairn describes a self besieged by "inner saboteurs"—voices of criticism, guilt, anxiety, and rage. His definition of pathology as the "relationship of the ego to its internalized objects" presupposes an ego strong enough to interact with these internal objects and not be continually (although perhaps occasionally) overwhelmed by them. Kohut, on the other hand, portrays a self that lacks a sense of cohesion, structure, and what he calls a "core nuclear program," or basic sense of direction. Fairbairn's paradigmatic patient needs to be free from what he or she has internalized; Kohut's paradigmatic patient needs more internalizations in order to develop more psychic structure.

Transference or object relations are the core of personality and psychopathology. But here Kohut takes a decisive step beyond Fairbairn and makes relationships the core of treatment as well. Psychopathology results from the empathic failures of childhood that block the development of selfhood. But if experiences of empathy are provided later on, the process of self-development can resume. The image that guides Kohut's theory of treatment is that of "thwarted and remobilized self development responding to self development–thwarting and self development–enhancing selfobjects" (1984:142). Therapy, then, provides a developmental second chance.

This leads to a revision of the goals of treatment. In Kohut's words: "We define therapeutic progress toward mental health not primarily by reference to expanded knowledge or increased ego autonomy, but by reference to the laying down of permanent self structures" (1984:153). And the necessity of empathic selfobject relations for developing a sense of self leads to a radical transformation of the nature of treatment. In answer to the question that is the title of his book "How does analysis cure?" Kohut suggests that the analyst provides the patient with the selfobject experiences needed to grow new psychic structures. Thus the agent of change is not interpretation and insight but the relationship itself, "the opening of a path of empathy between self and selfobject, specifically the establishment of empathic in-tuneness between self and selfobject" (1984:66).

The popularity of Kohut's work is itself a piece of data relevant to the heuristic power of his theories. Presumably his experientially rich descriptions of the fragmented and fragile self and its need for understanding and acceptance carry an empathic resonance with much human experience in modern culture. Kohut's theory of selfobjects itself clearly functions as a selfobject for many.

## Merton Gill

In contrast to Freud, Merton Gill's 1979 paper on "The Analysis of the Transference" represents the transference of analysis from a focus on the genetic past to the interactive present.

The Newtonian science of Freud's day, atomism, was the science of discrete particles bullied about by a few simple forces. Just as the billiard balls of matter could be separated from each other and the forces that acted on them, so scientists could be seen as separate from the objects of their research—hence the myth of objectivity with its aloof and detached observer-scientist, a spectator on the world whose observations failed to disturb the forces and interactions going on beneath his or her gaze. Freud's model of transference depended upon a strict atomistic distinction between doctor and patient. Freud called this fundamental principle "neutrality," a scientific paradigm transformed into a therapeutic technique in which the aloof and uninvolved scientist became the aloof and uninvolved analyst whose presence did not disturb the forces going on in the patient.

Gill is certain that no such separation of analyst and analysand is possible.

> No matter how far the analyst attempts to carry this limitation of his behavior, the very existence of the analytic situation provides the patient with innumerable cues which inevitably become his rationale for his transference responses. . . . [Thus there is an] inevitable intertwining of the transference with the current situation. . . . If the analyst remains under the

illusion that the current cues he provides to the patient can be reduced to the vanishing point, he may be led into a silent withdrawal. . . . The patient's responses under such conditions can be mistaken for unconscious transference when they are in fact transference adaptations to the actuality of the silence. (1979:271)

For Gill transference is always interaction. It is a myth that the analyst's behavior contributes nothing to the patient's response.

Thus, according to Gill, transference interpretations should be primarily focused on the interaction of patient and therapist, not on the projections of genetic material onto a supposedly blank screen. Analysis becomes the examination of the actual patterns of interaction between patient and analyst in the "here and now." This "respects the patient's efforts to be plausible and realistic rather than seeing him as manufacturing his attitudes out of whole cloth" (1979:273).

The Newtonian postulate of a world out there totally distinct from all observers had been the cornerstone of Freud's system, the "reality principle." A metaphysical claim now became a diagnostic rule, for it was under the hegemony of the reality principle that truth was distinguished from illusion, sanity from insanity. Such a principle was crucial to the interpretation of the transference, for the patient had to be persuaded by the analyst that he or she was distorting the "reality" of the analyst by projecting childhood material. Of course, any comments at all about the analyst were, of necessity, projections and distortions since the "reality" of the analyst was presumably that of a blank screen.

Gill broke the spell of the myth of objectivity under which Freud labored. Especially in the interpersonal sphere (although quantum mechanics suggests this is also true of the physical world) there is no reality apart from our relation to it and that relationship affects the reality we are observing. With the myth of objective reality refuted, analyzing the transference shifts from uncovering reality to interpreting it. Analysis, then, becomes a collaborative effort in which "analyst and patient engage in a dialogue in the spirit of attempting to arrive at a consensus about reality" (1979:274). This moves Gill toward the camp of those who seek to redefine psychoanalysis as a hermeneutical discipline (see also Spence 1982; Messer, Sass, and Woolfolk 1988).

In this collaborative effort, the focus is on the patient's responding to cues in the present, rather than on how she or he is repeating instinctual patterns from the past. Transference, then, is an ongoing cybernetic process in which Gill recognizes that "transference interpretations . . . have an effect on the transference" (1979:277). This line of thinking moves Gill away from Freud's Newtonian model of an inert analyst observing a self-contained, intrapsychic interplay of forces (called the patient) toward the conception of analyst and patient as parts of a single reciprocal system called the transference.

### Robert Stolorow, Frank Lachmann, and George Atwood

In a series of papers, one of which is provocatively entitled "Transference: The Future of an Illusion," Stolorow, Lachmann, and Atwood articulate a model of transference based on the conviction that "the organization of experience is a central motive in the patterning of human action" (Stolorow and Atwood 1984:99). This theory of motivation as the organizing of experience becomes the core of a theory of personality in which personality is defined as "the structure of a person's experiencing. Thus the basic units for our investigations of personality are the structures of experience—the distinctive configurations of self and object that shape and organize a person's subjective world. . . . Such structures of subjectivity are disclosed in the thematic patterning of a person's subjective life" (98). In keeping with this model of personality, the goal of psychoanalytic understanding is not uncovering the childhood instinctual roots of human behavior but rather illuminating "the structure, significance, origins, and therapeutic transformations of personal subjective worlds in all their richness and diversity" (87).

Rather than a Newtonian experiment in which the observer-analyst studies the object-patient, psychoanalysis "may be conceptualized as an intersubjective process involving a dialogue between two personal universes. The goal of this dialogue is the illumination of the inner pattern of one life—that distinctive structure of meanings that brings together the different parts of an individual's world in an intelligible whole" (Stolorow and Atwood 1984:91).

The task of metapsychology is not the discovery of objective entities that form the building blocks of human personality and human behavior (be they egos, ids, and superegos or schedules of reinforcement) but rather the specification of "a methodological system of interpretive principles to guide the study of meaning in human experience and conduct" (Stolorow and Atwood 1984:99). Given the primacy of the individual's "personal subjective world" (87), the goal of psychoanalysis becomes grasping the themes governing that personal world and showing how the rest of the person's life (their ideas, behaviors, wishes, and fears) expresses that personal universe. (For example, in their fascinating study, *Faces in a Cloud* [1979], Stolorow and Atwood trace the origins of Freud's and Jung's theories of personality to the personalities of Freud and Jung.)

It must be kept in mind that the fundamental locus of this theory is not epistemology and hermeneutics as much as it may sound that way. Rather, Stolorow, Lachmann, and Atwood's primary concern is clinical psychoanalysis, especially the psychoanalytic treatment of psychotic patients. The bridge between this epistemic theory of personality and the analysis of schizophrenics lies in Kohut's theory of the centrality of empathy in human life. The lack of empathic resonance leads to psychopathology (and the earlier and more severe this lack, the greater the damage), and the creation of an empathic relationship, in Stolorow and Lachmann's words, "serves to reinstate developmental processes that had been aborted during the patient's formative years" (Stolorow and Lachmann 1980:104).

Empathy, then, becomes the primary psychoanalytic technique:

> It is essential to the psychoanalytic treatment of psychotic patients that the therapist strive to comprehend the core of subjective truth symbolically encoded in the patient's delusional ideas and to communicate this understanding in a form the patient can use. Consistent empathic decoding of the patient's subjective truth gradually establishes the therapeutic bond as an archaic intersubjective context in which his belief in his own personal reality can become more firmly consolidated. . . . the only reality that is relevant and accessible to psychoanalytic inquiry is subjective reality—that of the patient, that of the analyst, and the psychological field created by the interplay between the two. (Stolorow, Brandchaft, and Atwood 1985:np)

Empathy, then, is the process of understanding another's personal subjective world from the "inside," so to speak.

Psychoanalytic understanding is, in itself, curative, but not because it gives the patient intellectual insight into his or her repressed drives. For Lachmann, Stolorow, and Atwood, understanding is never purely intellectual. Rather psychoanalytic understanding is inherently relational. It involves an "archaic bond with the analyst as selfobject" (Stolorow and Lachmann 1980:104). Empathic understanding is the very essence of that bond. Its presence mobilizes the blocked developmental processes of the patient (Stolorow and Lachmann 1985:33). Grasping another's personal subjective world is no abstract philosophical enterprise but rather the most powerful remedial agent known to psychology.

Within this framework, the transference is one more example of this "universal psychological striving to organize experience and construct meanings" (Stolorow and Lachmann 1985:27). As he does throughout his life, the patient makes sense of the analytic experience in terms of his major organizing themes and "assimilates the analytic relationship into the thematic structures of his personal subjective world. . . . [Transference is] an expression of the continuing influence of organizing principles and imagery that crystallized out of the patient's early formative experiences" (26).

Stolorow and Lachmann (1985) agree with Freud that transference is a form of repetition. But what are repeated are not basic biological satisfactions or ambivalent feelings but rather patterns of organizing experience. "The persistence of transference is . . . the result of the continuing influence of established organizing principles" (29). Thus the transference does give the therapist insight into the patient's childhood—that is, into the organizing themes that governed (and still govern) the patient's subjective world.

> Insight into the patient's early history is possible not because an idea from the past has been displaced to the present but because the structures that were organized in the past continue to be functionally effective or remain available for periodic mobilization. . . . these themes have either remained overtly salient throughout the patient's life . . . or have been providing a more subtle background organization. (23)

The analysis of the transference is the analysis neither of the patient's defenses against instinctual impulses nor of her patterns of relationship in the present. Rather the analysis focuses on the ways in which the patient organizes her experience and structures her subjective world.

As with Gill, a Newtonian model of objectivity—in which the analyst presumably knows in some unimpeachable way what is going on in the transference—is eschewed. There are

> certain dangers embedded in the concept of a "real" relationship between analyst and patient, of which the transference is presumed to be a distortion. Such dangers lie in the fact that judgments about what is "really true" about the analyst and what is distortion of that "truth" are ordinarily left solely to the discretion of the analyst—hardly a disinterested party. . . . therapists often invoke the concept of distortion when the patient's feelings . . . contradict self-perceptions and expectations that the therapist requires for his own well-being. (Stolorow and Lachmann 1985:25)

The Newtonian metaphor of separate entities bound by linear causality meets the same fate. "The therapeutic relationship is always shaped by both inputs from the analyst and the structures of meaning into which these are assimilated by the patient." Neutrality is no longer the austere isolation of the analyst but is redefined to mean empathy— "understanding of the patient's expressions from within the perspective of the patient's subjective frame of reference" (Stolorow and Lachmann 1985:32).

Although the three men continually acknowledge their debt to Kohut, it should be noted in passing that their emphasis is rather different than his. Stolorow, Lachmann, and Atwood give priority to the personal subjective world, whereas Kohut begins from the centrality of the interpersonal world. Thus they define empathy as an appreciation of the primacy of subjectivity, whereas Kohut speaks of empathy in interpersonal terms, as a bond or a relationship. For whatever reasons, theirs is a reading of Kohut structured around themes of the importance of subjectivity and privacy rather than themes of connection and interaction. It is Kohut for the introverted.

Empathy replaces neutrality. Intersubjective interaction replaces Freud's Lockean image of the analyst as a tabula rasa for the patient's projections. And transference "refers neither to regression, displacement, projection, nor distortion," but is rather "an expression of the universal psychological striving to organize experience and create meanings" (Stolorow and Lachmann 1985:35).

## The Deep Structure of Relationships

Since Freud, transference and repetition have been virtually interchangeable. It comes as no surprise to clinicians or to any self-aware person that patterns tend to repeat in people's lives, often to their detriment. Theories of transference are also attempts at explaining this often all-too-common and all-too-painful phenomenon. To Freud, patterns repeat because biological drives continually strive for satisfaction and because we continually project the same ambivalent wishes and feelings onto the people and situations in our environment. As noted before, this is a theory of linear causality in which instincts cause projections and projections cause people and situations to look and feel all too familiar.

Post-Freudian commentators have found this paradigm too simplistic and have tended to substitute models of reciprocal systems and mutual interactions. The implication of many of these newer models is that just as it is a *relationship* that is internalized, it is a *relationship* that is reenacted in the transference proper and throughout our lives. We repeat these patterns in order to replay and reexperience significant relationships and roles.

Several schools of psychotherapy have made use of this insight. For example, James Framo has attempted to apply this vision to marital and family therapy. Framo believes that adopting an object relations perspective requires a radical revision of our model of human nature: "man is viewed not as a personality constellation with defined limits but as being linked to, shaped by, and shaping the natural habitat within which he is involved" (1970:301). In different terms, this is the same epistemic shift from the primacy of the atomized individual to the priority of a system of interactions found in Kohut's self psychology. It is striking that the two most powerful psychological theories of the second half of this century—family therapy and self psychology—both shift the focus from the isolated individual to the interactional system. (For a discussion of the theoretical development of family therapy, see Hoffman [1981]. A parallel shift has been occurring at the same time in physics and the philosophy of science [see Jones 1984].)

In an article deeply indebted to Fairbairn, "Symptoms from a Family Transactional Viewpoint," Framo begins with the now familiar claim that it is "the emotional relationship between the self and some external object which is internalized." This relationship is re-created in marriages and families, for "active, unconscious attempts are made to force and change close relationships into fitting the internal role models" (1970:274, 275).

But since the bad object is often unconscious, we may deal with it by the process that Klein and Fairbairn call "projective identification" and unload the unconscious and unwanted internalized object onto those closest to us. Framo writes, "Spouses attribute to the partner those bad feelings they must not own in themselves or else make the partner all good while they themselves [are] taking on the badness" (1970:276). Thus current networks and families may come to look and feel and even act like our original ones. Is this simply because we cunningly pick others who will easily fit the roles of our inner drama or are our projections so powerful that they distort our perception of the other and we lose sight of the person's reality? Certainly both these things can and do happen in intimate relationships. But might not some other process be at work as well?

In a fascinating paper, "Induced Emotional Reactions and Attitudes in the Psychoanalyst as Transference in Actuality," the psychoanalyst Alan Roland attempts to answer precisely that question. By induced reactions, Roland means "emotional reactions and attitudes in the psychoanalyst based on the patient's unconscious need to actualize or recreate the analyst in experience as the internalized parental imago (internal object or object-representation) or some aspect of the self-representation through the patient subtly evoking a whole range of emotional reactions and attitudes in the analyst" (Roland 1981:48). Roland wants to distinguish these "induced reactions" from the Freudian notion of countertransference. The classical view of countertransference, like the transference itself, depended on the Newtonian images of separate entities and linear causality; only now there was a causal projection from analyst to patient as well as from patient to analyst. In the classical definition of countertransference, Roland writes, "patient and analyst are viewed as being essentially separate and distinct . . . thus maintaining the essential Cartesian dualism of the psychoanalytic relationship, as well as of psychoanalytic theory," and so "the widely held, unquestioned assumption that all of the patient's reactions are transference has been conceptually extended to the analyst, thus labelling all the analyst's reactions as countertransference" (49, 62).

It is, however, no longer possible to maintain that neat and tidy separation since the basic units of psychological life are relationships, not isolated objects. The core of the argument is the claim that "internalizations consist not simply of parental imagoes alone, but rather of patterned interactions between child and parent, or parents, or even of the total family. Thus, transference displacements and projections are based on internalized patterns of relationships involving self and object representations" (Roland 1981:50). So, whereas "transference has classically been considered to be unconscious displacements . . . from the original parental imagoes and/or the projection of parental imagoes (internal objects) onto the analyst or others" (50), this is no longer tenable because internalizations are not discrete objects or images of objects but rather interactional patterns. The individual takes in her family. The interior life is a family meeting going on inside her head. Transference, then, is not the projection and/or reexperiencing of repressed impulses but rather the actual re-creation of these relational patterns.

In an induced reaction, the analyst, or any person, starts to live the part which the patient is projecting on him. "The analyst through his emotional reactions and attitudes becomes the transference object in actuality rather than through projections. . . . He actually starts having the feelings and attitudes of the role" (1988:51). The analyst, or some other significant person, may feel anger toward the patient or a desire to criticize him—feelings the patient may be inducing in the analyst from out of the patient's lived experience. "I was working with a man," Roland writes, "who had unconsciously internalized his mother's masterful way of arousing intense feelings of guilt in others, including me" (1981:66).

Induced reactions, then, function in two ways. First, they get the analyst to undergo the feelings of anger, shame, guilt, anxiety, and so on associated with patients' experiences during their early years. Roland suggests that

> the actual emotions and attitudes of the parent can be internalized, in contrast to the almost ubiquitous emphasis on the introjection of the object . . . the semi-autonomous form of these presences and the enormous intra-psychic influences they have, often being experienced by patients as foreign bodies that wield tremendous power over them. . . . Patients have unconscious presences of actual parental emotional attitudes that wield enormous influences on their lives. (1981:68)

In an induced reaction the analyst begins to feel what the parents felt toward the patient as a child or what the patient felt as a child in relation to the parents.

Second, induced reactions re-create relational patterns from the past, sometimes with patient and therapist playing several roles. Such episodes involve the "reconstruction of deeply internalized parent-child interactions, and of crucial, unconscious parental attitudes and emotional states and their effects on the patient" (1981:58).

Psychopathology, then, results from the internalization of these destructive patterns of relationship in which "the disturbed familial relationship penetrates the patient's ego boundaries and becomes internalized" (1981:56). These disturbed familial relationships then get played out not only in the inner world (with Fairbairn's internal saboteurs) but also in the outer world through the repetition of these patterns in actual relationships. Thus the repetition that occurs in the transference and throughout people's lives may "constitute a subtle reliving of a critical introject" (1981:52). Again, by an introject, Roland means "the introjection of the particular non-empathic or emotionally unrelated aspects of the parental personality" (1981:67)—not a discrete object but a certain experience of relatedness (or nonrelatedness).

In the therapeutic relationship and in all intimate relationships a person is expressing the deep structure of her personality, enacting into the external world those patterns of affect and interaction that constitute her inner world. For it seems that these patterns, once internalized, cannot remain totally inward but push for expression and reenactment in the external world as well. Since the basic units of selfhood are not

31

instinctual drives, beliefs, assumptions, or emotions but patterns of interaction, the analysis of the transference means coming to understand the ways in which all human activities display this deep structure of human personality.

## Post-Freudian Theories: Summary

Contemporary psychoanalytic models of transference agree with Freud that transference is a ubiquitous human phenomenon. Such a postulate is necessary in order for the analytic relationship to be seen as indicative of and therefore mutative for patterns occurring in the rest of the patient's life. But such ubiquity is grounded not in the demand of biological drives to be satisfied but rather in the inevitability of relationships, the universal need to make sense of our experience, and the deep structure of the psyche as internalized patterns of interaction. Such newer models of transference are part of the movement away from Freud's biological determinism.

Freud thought in the language of discrete atoms and linear causality, so inevitably he conceived of the transference as involving two separate parties, one actively affecting the other who remains unmoved and objective. Contemporary commentators are more inclined to see reciprocal interactions where Freud saw linear causes. Thus the transference becomes a mutual system of interactions. And the individual is repositioned from his Newtonian loneliness to existing always in relation to a larger world of people and experiences. The focus thus shifts from an analysis of the individual's defenses against instincts to an analysis of patterns of interaction. Newer models of transference are part of the movement away from the Newtonian world picture that governed science in Freud's day.

Post-Freudian models of personality and transference also help locate contemporary psychoanalysis in the context of other complementary changes in modern culture (Jones 1982). Physics no longer describes the foundations of matter in terms of discrete particles but rather in terms of patterns of interaction (Jones 1984). General systems theory—to which we will return several times in this book—is having a wide influence in the biological and social sciences (Hoffman 1981; Jones 1986). The theme of the relational self has been picked up by many feminist authors (Chodorow 1989; Flax 1990); perhaps if psychoanalysis had been invented by a woman it would look something like Kohut's self psychology or other interpersonal paradigms.

Similarly with the psychoanalytic study of religion: Freud's biological determinism and Newtonian atomism set the terms in which he analyzed religion. The next chapter will show how a new set of terms and a new understanding of psychoanalysis make possible a rather different treatment of religion.

# CHAPTER

## 2

### TRANSFERENCE
### AND
### TRANSCENDENCE

Understanding the transference, then, has implications far beyond undoing the repression of instincts. Analyzing the transference also means comprehending how experiences are assimilated into and function within the patient's characteristic styles of making meaning and relating to the world and how the person's behavior expresses the internalized relational structures of his or her personality. These different theoretical approaches to the transference also have important consequences for a psychoanalytic investigation of religion. Their import can be demonstrated through comparison with other psychoanalytic studies of religion, several of which will be surveyed below.

### *Sigmund Freud*

Freud's model of the transference as repetition would lead the psychoanalytic investigator to look for the historical roots of religion. This is exactly what Freud did, focusing on the history of the individual in *The Future of an Illusion* and the history of "mankind" in *Totem and Taboo*. Congruent with Freud's model of transference is his definition of understanding as seeking and finding historical origins. This was a method he applied with particular consistency to religion, writing, "A little boy is bound to love and admire his father, who seems to him the most powerful, the kindest and the wisest creature in the world. God himself is after all only an exaltation of this picture of the father as he is represented in the mind of early childhood" (1914:243). For Freud, then, religion is another form of transference, and, like all transference phenomena, it is but a replay of childhood.

What is replayed is the chronic instinctual warfare that governs all human activities. The roots of religion, like all the neuroses, lay in the oedipal triangle. As I noted earlier, in *Totem and Taboo* Freud located the origin of religion in the history of the primal horde of sons who kill the primal father because he has prohibited sexual relations with the women of the clan. Thus is the oedipal drama enacted in the childhood of mankind. The evil deed is repressed but it returns as guilt. The need to overcome this guilt through reconciliation with the slain patriarch is projected first onto a totem animal and later onto a heavenly father.

This conviction that religion provides illusory conciliation remained unshaken throughout Freud's life, although he broadened it in *The Future of an Illusion* to include our reconciliation to the terrors of nature, the tragedy of death, and the repressions of society. The child within us may wish for a blissful state in which oedipal ambivalence is transcended, but the rational adult can only renounce those infantile fantasies of paradise and resign himself to the unresponsiveness of matter, the finality of death, and the necessity of self-denial.

## William Meissner

A thorough and searching analysis of Freud's treatment of religion is conducted by William Meissner in his 1984 book, *Psychoanalysis and Religious Experience*. In responding to Freud's attack on religion, Meissner makes three basic moves: (1) as Leavy puts it, Meissner "turn[s] the psychoanalytic tables on Freud" (1988:87) by applying the same psychoanalytic methods to Freud's atheism that Freud applied to religion; (2) Meissner draws on the post-Freudian developments of Hartmann (1958) and ego psychology to argue that religion can be ego-adaptive as well as neurotic; and (3) Meissner suggests that religion represents what

Winnicott (1971) calls "transitional phenomena" and thus has a positive role to play in the individual's life.

After describing Freud's antireligious arguments in depth, Meissner applies these same arguments to Freud's atheism, concluding that "there can be little doubt that Freud's religious views . . . reflected at every step deep psychological forces and unresolved conflicts within his psychic economy" (1984:55). Meissner documents that Freud himself possessed a strong superstitious streak that he was constantly denying and defending himself against. "It seems clear," he writes, "that Freud's unresolved mystical trends were being projected and dealt with in an externalized form" (1984:55), especially in Freud's attacks on religion and on Jung's mystical tendencies. In addition, Freud's ambivalence toward his Jewish heritage is well documented (see, for example, Cuddihy 1974; Rainey 1975; Robert 1976; Van Herik 1982); it was an unresolved ambivalence, which Meissner shows runs through all his writings on religion whether or not they deal with Judaism. Thus, Meissner concludes:

> As we have seen, Freud's interweaving of these complex [religious] themes rides on a powerful undercurrent that stems from unresolved infantile conflicts. Deep in the recesses of his mind, Freud seems to have resolved that his truculent spirit would never yield to the demands of religion for submission and resignation. He would be a Hannibal, a conquistador—and a Moses, a prophet who would find a new religion that would enable him to lead his people to the Promised Land of psychological freedom. But the only way for him to achieve this goal required that he overcome the religion of his fathers and annihilate the very image of the father himself. . . . Freud was never able to free himself from these deep-seated entanglements and their associated conflicts, and ultimately what he taught us about religion, religious experience, and faith must be taken in the context of these unconscious conflicts. (1984:55–56)

As Rizzuto (1979) says, for Freud atheism was normative; the mature person was ipso facto an atheist. Only religious conviction required further explanation and analysis. Although Freud conceded that psychoanalysis could not pass on the truth claims of religion but only its psychological function, he remained adamant that religion was false because it had no place in reality as seen through the eyes of Newtonian science. So convinced was he, on these grounds, of the falsity of religion that he failed to notice that just as there can be a psychoanalysis of belief, so there can be a psychoanalysis of unbelief. Just as there are neurotic reasons for believing in God, so there are neurotic reasons for refusing belief. Such a psychoanalysis of unbelief is thoroughly conducted by Meissner, using Freud himself as a case history, and later we will examine the case of a man who was also an atheist and explore the psychodynamics of his atheism but from a rather different perspective.

Meissner also responds to Freud's argument on its own terms, suggesting that a psychoanalytic examination discloses other functions that religion performs besides the neurotic ones that Freud discusses. For Freud, the primary function of the ego was control of the instincts: "where id is, let ego be" was the Freudian maxim. Certain post-Freudian theoreticians, particularly Heinz Hartmann (1958), argued that the ego is not only the creation of the conflict between the id and reality; it is also autonomous, having functions of its own undetermined by instinctual pressures. From this point of view, one can analyze religion in terms of how it contributes to or undermines such tasks as mastery or adaption. "Understanding religious dynamism," Meissner writes, "must be cast in the more evolved contemporary theory of ego functioning. The conception of religion as a neurotic adaption to infantile wishes then shifts to that of a more positive adaptive function of the ego" (1984:132).

Hartmann proposed, for example, that sanity and maturity require a moral ordering of life, a set of values to guide and sustain action. Without it, life disintegrates into chaos and discontinuity (Hartmann 1960). The more complex life becomes, the more complex and differentiated the moral code that guides it must become. For Freud, religious morality was entirely a function of the superego with its harsh and unrealistic (and therefore neurotic) demands. For Hartmann and Meissner, belief in a religiously based moral order may also be lodged in the ego and "can be seen as a creative effort to reinforce and sustain the more highly organized and integrated adaptational concerns. These concerns depend in large measure on the capacity of the ego for adaptive symbolic organization of experience" (Meissner 1984:131). Similarly, religion has helped fulfill the human requirements for meaning and identity of which Erickson (1968) as well as Hartmann have spoken.

Meissner summarizes his discussion of the functions of religion by saying, "The picture that emerges from these reflections is of the development of man's religious enterprise as an adaptive effort of the ego in the face of the multiple and fundamental challenges to its integrity and vitality. . . . The religious concern may serve as a vital psychological force that supports the individual in his attempts at self-definition and realization" (1984:133)—a point for which Gordon Allport argued in *The Individual and His Religion* (1950).

Meissner, in responding to Freud's attack on religion, draws on the work of Winnicott (1971). Freud, he said, cast his discoveries in the language he had at hand—that of Newtonian science with its materialistic and mechanistic models. Thus a central pillar of Freud's intellectual edifice was the reality principle, a metaphysical idea used as a diagnostic category. And the "reality" behind the reality principle was the physical world as described by nineteenth-century physics. Armed with this definition of what could be true and what had to be false, what could be real and what had to be imaginary, Freud could easily attack religion and philosophy as the products of faulty thinking and imagination.

In a series of papers describing what he calls "transitional objects and transitional phenomena," Winnicott (1971) tries to soften Freud's hard and fast distinction between reality and hallucination by staking out an "intermediate area of *experiencing*, to which inner reality and external life both contribute . . . the intermediate area between the subjective and what is objectively perceived" (1971:2–3). Winnicott continues to refer to this phenomenon by Freud's term *illusion*. Such usage may create some confusion because he does not mean it in Freud's carefully delineated sense of illusion as expressing the pleasure principle (Freud [1927] 1964). Thus Winnicott finds it hard to remove the ordinary connotation of something unreal and totally subjective that clings to the term *illusion* (see Leavy 1986; Loewald 1988). But Winnicott's intention is clearly to reframe "illusory experience" from something suspect to something positive, as the origin of all creativity and culture.

Transitional phenomena begin with the infant's experience of the mother. Winnicott argues that this experience first focuses on the mother's body, and especially her breast, and later is carried by specific "transitional objects," like blankets and teddy bears, that continue to evoke the maternal experience of soothing and nurturance. Such objects smooth the infant's transition from dependence on (in Freud's terms) the pleasure principle of infantile wishes to acceptance of the reality principle. Because he was a pediatrician before he became a psychoanalyst, Winnicott had an extended opportunity to observe the child's use of such objects to ease the movement out of the maternal matrix and into the larger and less responsive objective world. Thus transitional objects are primarily defined by their use in this specific function. Besides blankets and teddy bears, other transitional phenomena identified by Winnicott include the capacity to play (1971:38–64; which Meissner calls the "capacity for blending illusion and reality" [1984:170]), the exercise of creativity (65–86), and the use of symbols and therefore the production of art, literature, and the entire range of human culture. All of these involve using "objects and phenomena from external reality . . . in the service of some sample derived from inner or personal reality" (51).

Meissner draws on Winnicott's notion of transitional phenomena and follows his lead in applying it to religion. But whereas Winnicott speaks of religion only in general terms, Meissner focuses on four aspects— faith, God representations, symbols, and prayer—treating them as transitional phenomena. Unlike Winnicott, he does not emphasize the *functions* of transitional phenomena in providing comfort and evoking the capacity for play, symbolization, creativity, and other activities carried on in what Winnicott calls "the transitional space." Rather, Meissner emphasizes the interplay of subjective and objective factors in the constellation of transitional phenomena, perhaps because he is seeking a viable location for religion, which for him belongs neither to the totally objective domain of physical objects in the world of space and time nor to the purely subjective world of hallucination and daydream.

"The faith experience has a number of attributes that characterize it as a form of transitional experience," Meissner writes. Like all transitional phenomena, faith "represents a realm in which the subjective and the objective interpenetrate." Although the believer brings personal and subjective experience to the process of believing, faith is not purely subjective. Its contents are grounded in the traditions and experiences of others in an organized community and relate to the nature of the world, of human existence, and of value and the presence of the spiritual realm. Thus, Meissner concludes, "both the subjective and objective poles of experience contribute to the substance of belief" (1984:178). (A more extensive exploration of the process of faith from a contemporary psychoanalytic perspective can be found in McDargh [1983] and a more philosophical discussion of the subjectivity of faith can be found in Jones [1981].)

In speaking of the psychodynamics of the God representation, Meissner relies heavily on the research of Ana-Maria Rizzuto (1979) whose work I will discuss in depth later. In keeping with his emphasis on transitional phenomena as bridging the gap between subjectivity and objectivity, Meissner writes, quoting Winnicott, that the God representation is neither purely subjective, like a hallucination, nor "is it totally beyond the reach of subjectivity; rather it is located, in Winnicott's terms 'outside, inside, at the border'" (1984:179). The individual's God representation emerges from the tension between her own private experience and the images and metaphors for God provided by her culture. It belongs neither to the individual's private world nor to the surrounding religious environment but is rather a synthesis of the two.

Another aspect of the religious life that Meissner labels as transitional is the use of physical, artistic, and linguistic objects to convey a spiritual or moral meaning. The crucifix, the Star of David, ritual gestures and vestments, sacred texts and phrases, holy shrines—all involve objects in the world of space and time but they are, for the believer, not only physical and temporal. They "are not to be envisioned merely in terms of their physical attributes. The crucifix is not just a piece of carved wood, nor the Torah simply a roll of parchment with ancient writing on it" (Meissner 1984:181). To describe the botanical species of tree from which a crucifix is carved or the chemical composition of the ink used to inscribe the Torah is to miss the believer's point. The cross is made from wood and the Torah from ink, but in a religious context they become vehicles for meanings that go beyond botany and calligraphy.

Meissner is content to call such symbolization "transitional" because "the objects as religious symbols are neither exclusively perceived in real and objective terms nor simply produced by subjective creation. Rather, they evolve from the amalgamation of what is real, material, and objective as it is experienced, penetrated, and creatively reshaped by the subjective belief and patterns of meaning attributed to the object by the believer" (1984:181).

Meissner alludes to but does not discuss in detail a point to which I will return later: what makes such objects religious (and transitional in some sense) is not just that the believer attributes his subjective religious (and psychological) meaning to these physical things but also that they are used in the context of a certain psychological space or state of consciousness. It is not just that certain words or gestures or things become associated with certain religious ideas but that "such symbols become part of the transitional realm of the believer's illusory experience" (1984:181). As should be clear by now, I think Meissner's use of the term *illusory* only confuses the point, but it is in keeping with Winnicott's own usage. (The final chapter of this book will discuss in more depth the psychological and religious processes that go into the constellation of such religious symbols, drawing on the work of the theologian Paul Tillich and the psychoanalyst Christopher Bollas as well as on Winnicott's idea of transitional experience.)

Faith, God representations, and symbols, then, stand at the interface of subjective and objective worlds. The fourth form of religious experience Meissner mentions is prayer, the most "direct, immediate, and personal" type of religious experience. In his brief discussion of prayer, Meissner underscores the experiential locus of all transitional phenomena. They involve not only specific objects—blankets, teddy bears, fingers—but, more important, a specific psychological space or state of consciousness: "In prayer the individual figuratively enters the transitional space where he meets his God representation. . . . it shares the quality of transitional experience and expresses another aspect of the illusory dimension of religious experience" (1984:182).

Meissner's tendency, throughout his discussion of "religion as transitional" (the title of chapter 7), is to treat the term *transitional* as if it were primarily a predicate of certain objects (and Winnicott certainly does use it that way). But for Meissner the predicate mainly refers to objects that stand on the boundary between external and internal, objective and subjective, whereas for Winnicott it also refers to objects that perform a certain function and soothe the self in its transition from the world of infantile subjectivity to the world of adult objectivity. Meissner's brief discussion of prayer brings to light another use of the term. In prayer there really is no "object" that the believer manipulates but rather a psychological "space" or state of consciousness that she enters. And from a religious standpoint that may be the most significant referent of the term *transitional*.

The recognition that dynamic (and neurotic) factors similar to those operative in religion can also play a part in atheism, the elaboration of the adaptive as well as infantile functions of religion, and the undercutting of Freud's rigid dualism of objectivity and subjectivity through use of Winnicott's category of transitional phenomena—all enable Meissner both to remain loyal to Freud's single-minded focus on the psychological dynamics underlying religious experience and to move beyond Freud's critical evaluation of those dynamics.

### Ana-Maria Rizzuto

Among psychoanalytic investigators who have approached religion in terms of the process of object relations is Ana-Maria Rizzuto. In a pioneering study entitled *The Birth of the Living God,* she investigated "the possible origins of the individual's private representation of God" (1979:3). Rizzuto collected information on the family, developmental history, and religious convictions of several psychiatric patients and then had them draw pictures of their families and their gods. From this project she proposed several theses:

1. The child internalizes his interactions with the world in terms of a variety of "object representations." These are complex phenomena that may include, among other things, somatic sensations, affects, and concepts.

2. These discrete memories are consolidated into ever more complex sets of representations. For example, an internal representation of the child's mother may be an amalgamation of sensations of being held and rocked, the sound of her voice and the feelings it generated, and the need to idealize her.

3. Every child is an implicit philosopher, wondering about the origin of the world, and each needs the idea of God to answer the question

"why?" The idea of God is developmentally necessary to ground our earliest awareness of the existence of things.

4. This representation of God is the apex of the process of consolidating object representations into a coherent inner object world; it is compounded out of the bits and pieces of object representations the child has at her disposal. God, Rizzuto says "is created from representational materials whose sources are the representations of primary objects" (1979:178).

Thus the child's development of a cohesive sense of self may make use of a representation of God to mirror and focus the self's integrative processes. Just as cognitively religion often functions as the most general heuristic schema the person uses to make sense of his or her life experience (Jones 1972), so psychologically religion serves to consolidate the bits and pieces of a person's inner representational world. The term *religion* comes from the Latin word *religio,* which means, among other things, "to bind together." And both philosophically and psychodynamically, religion binds experiences together. Thus Rizzuto writes that "the sense of self is in fact in dialectical interaction with a God representation that has become essential to the maintenance of the sense of being oneself" (1979:5).

She uses Kohut's concepts of a mirroring transference and a selfobject bond to explain the early creation of the God representation out of the experience of the mother (1979:185–188). Our earliest sense of self, she suggests, grows from seeing our self mirrored in our mother's reactions. If the mirror is cracked or darkened, our sense of self will be distorted. For Rizzuto, this early experience of mirroring, which forms the basis of a cohesive sense of self, lies at the core of our God representation. All other images that are joined to it in the elaboration of our private God representation are colored by that core mirroring experience (or lack of it) with the mother.

One significant and controversial implication of Rizzuto's work is that everyone, of necessity, forms some internal god representation in order to end the infinite regress of questions about the origin of the world and to consolidate the representational fragments born of his or her early life. The representation is there whether or not the person, as Rizzuto says, "uses it for belief" (1979:200). Often when students have spoken at great length with me about how they do not believe in God, I ask them to tell me about the God they do not believe in. *And they always answer.* They have a very clear idea of who or what God is, even though they don't believe in him. And I must observe in passing that their images are often of a God that I wouldn't believe in either. However cognitively compelling it may be, total atheism for Rizzuto is a psychodynamic impossibility. Everyone has some image of God, even if the person rejects it as an object of faith.

As we saw in the discussion of Meissner, Rizzuto follows Winnicott (1971) in explicitly locating the reality of God in the "transitional space," halfway between hallucination and physical reality. In this realm of the imagination, the child creates a private but real world of transitional objects—teddy bears, imaginary friends, security blankets, personal games, magical beliefs. Part of Rizzuto's book is a deliberate attempt to validate the importance of fantasy and the imagination for mental health, as opposed to Freud's empirical austerity (see, for example, Rizzuto 1979:46–53). God is, for Rizzuto, a creation of the imagination, but that is precisely the source of his power and reality. We cannot live without the creations of our imagination, and Rizzuto stresses their psychological importance.

> We have forgotten the powerful reality of nonexistent objects, objects of our creation. . . . The fictive creations of our minds . . . have as much regulatory potential in our psychic function as people around us in the flesh. . . . Human life is impoverished when these immaterial characters made out of innumerable experiences vanish under the repression of a psychic realism that does violence to the ceaseless creativity of the human mind. In this sense, at least, religion is not an illusion. It is an integral part of being human, truly human in our capacity to create nonvisible but meaningful realities. . . . Without those fictive realities human life becomes a dull animal existence. (1979:47)

By "real" Rizzuto clearly means powerful. Such "fictive" entities as "muses, guardian angels, heroes . . . the Devil, God himself . . . unseen atoms, imaginary chemical formulas" (1979:27) can have a powerful impact on human lives and their psychic power constitutes their reality. Imaginary playmates and abstract ideas perform an indispensable psychological function in the lives of individuals and cultures, and so the imaginative capacity demands respect rather than denigration.

I should mention that Rizzuto notices and remarks on a significant difference between God and all other transitional objects. The others are eventually outgrown and put away. As every parent knows, in the course of childhood, the closet literally overflows with discarded transitional objects—teddy bears, toys, bits of blankets, favored outfits. But, notes Rizzuto, God is not among them. In the normal course of things, the psychic history of God is the reverse of that of other transitional objects: "instead of losing meaning, God's meaning becomes heightened." Because God is a "nonexperiential" object and the God representation, unlike teddy bears and security blankets, is infinitely plastic, the person can throughout life " 'create' a God according to his needs" (1979:179).

It is worth questioning whether that is a sufficient explanation for this difference between God and the rest of the inhabitants of the transitional world. Winnicott, to whom Rizzuto is indebted for this argument, takes it in a slightly different direction. When speaking about transitional objects, Winnicott is really calling attention to a certain capacity for *experience*, writing that transitional phenomena point to "an intermediate area of *experiencing* to which inner reality and external reality both contribute" (1971:2). Teddy bears and security blankets are left behind, but the capacity to transcend the dichotomies of inner and outer, subjective and objective, continues to grow and becomes the basis for human creativity in the arts and sciences. Making a point I will return to several times, Winnicott writes that the transitional object "is not forgotten and it is not mourned. It loses meaning, and this is because the transitional phenomena have become diffused, have become spread out over the whole intermediate territory between inner psychic reality and the external world . . . that is to say, over the whole cultural field" (1979:14). Imagination represents more than world of ghosts and goblins and fairy tales; it is the source of the plays of Shakespeare and the formulae of Einstein (for more on the centrality of imagination in science, see Polanyi [1974] and Gerhart and Russell [1984]). Watching a child play with a teddy bear, Winnicott saw a child developing the capacity to write a novel or invent a machine or propose a theory.

Rizzuto focuses too much on the transitional *object* and not enough on the transitional *experience*. Thus she often makes God sound like a supernatural version of the teddy bear and then speculates on why the deity is not discarded like other such "objects." But what is important here is not an object but a capacity for experience and perhaps one's God is not discarded because it is the carrier of that capacity par excellence (a point to which I will return in the final chapter).

Rizzuto suggests that the God representation is reworked, added to, and transformed as the individual goes through life and brings new experiences to his or her inner representational world. Whether one becomes an atheist or a devotee is determined by whether or not one's image of God fits or can be reworked to fit one's needs at any given developmental stage. In Rizzuto's words, "Belief in God or its absence depends upon whether or not a conscious identity of experience can be established between the God representation of a given developmental moment and the object and self-representations needed to maintain a sense of self" (1979:202). For example, one of her subjects' image of God was so tinctured with masochistic anger and destructive rage (from the subject's experience with his father) that he was unable to make use of it as he grew up; he rejected any idea of God because the pain associated with it was intolerable.

Every developmental stage is also a crisis of belief since it demands that the God image be reworked to fit a new conception of self. If the God image is too brittle or rigid, it cannot be reworked and must be rejected in order for development to continue. As Rizzuto writes, her "central thesis is that God as a transitional representation needs to be recreated in each developmental crisis if it is to be found relevant for lasting belief" (1979:208). Other transitional objects are outgrown; given the potential plasticity of the idea of God, it can be continually refashioned and so need not be discarded as the person encounters new experiences requiring incorporation into his or her ever-developing sense of self. However fixed it may appear from the outside, internally the life of faith is an ongoing series of major and minor transformations and adjustments in the central image of God. Creedal formulations and ritual actions may remain unchanged from childhood to old age, but their inner meaning to the believer is continually being updated on the basis of new experiences.

Although referring to religion in terms of object relations, Rizzuto's language often contains the same ambiguity noted in reference to Fairbairn. Rizzuto frequently speaks of internalizations, including those relating to God, as "images," "object-representations," "objects," and "perceptual memories"—terms conveying an image of a tiny snapshot of the object within our heads. In keeping with this model of internalizations, much of her study is taken up with drawing connections between a patient's parental representations and the origins and transformations of his or her God representation. Although it is clear that the internalization of objects cannot be separated from our relationship with them, Rizzuto tends to focus more on the internalized objects themselves and less on the internalized relationships.

Despite their radically different starting points, in some ways Rizzuto's conclusions mirror Jung's. Religion is seen as a natural part of human development rather than a childhood stage to be outgrown. Thus humankind is, for both, *homo religiosus* (inherently religious) and religious conviction can be a sign of health as well as a symptom of pathology. For both the primary psychological function of the God imago or archetype is self-integration and cohesion.

### Stanley Leavy

Stanley Leavy takes as his starting point in *The Image of God* (1988) that image not in the object-relational sense used by Rizzuto and Meissner but in the biblical sense of the individual's personal center, thereby creating a more explicitly personal and theological set of reflections on psychoanalysis and religion than either Meissner or Rizzuto. Leavy feels that both psychoanalysis and theology concern themselves with uncovering the depths of human experience, and thus it is possible to "see an illuminating parallel between the psychoanalytic effort to disclose as much as possible of our deepest personal intentions and the ever-renewed Christian effort to show us the God who revealed and continues to reveal himself" (1988:56). Leavy wants to bring both psychoanalytic insight and theological wisdom to bear on such common human experiences as suffering, believing, and facing death.

Leavy is aware of the limits of the Newtonian natural scientific paradigm in a way that one could not expect Freud to have been, and he knows that "the positivism that restricts reality to the evidence of our senses falls far short of describing the human condition" (1988:91). He senses that the collapse of the positivism that governed Freud's work opens up again the question of religion's truth (a point I have made myself in a book [1981] on the philosophy of science and the philosophy of religion).

But what is to replace Freud's positivism? Leavy's reflections are informed by an understanding of psychoanalysis as a narrative discipline, an understanding he argues for in a 1980 book and that is articulated as well by Spence (1982), Schafer (1976), and, preeminently, Lacan (1978). Life themes have their own integrity, and psychoanalytic interpretation should focus on respecting and illuminating these themes and helping the patient forge them into a coherent narrative rather than explaining them as only the product of repressed desires. Thus an understanding of the psychoanalytic process as narrative allows analysis (and especially the analysis of religion) to be carried on in a nonreductive manner.

Armed with this hermeneutic, Leavy can agree with Freud that there is neurosis in religion without falling into the trap of saying that is all there is. The religious themes in a person's life—suffering, believing, dying—should be respected and can be illuminated by psychoanalysis. For example, having explored the dynamics of love and hate, Leavy suggests that "for me, loving and hating are the most revealing of all human capacities to resemble God as he has been revealed to us, and to depart from that resemblance" (1988:38). Or he writes that the experience of psychoanalysis "drives me to profound skepticism about our ability to take concrete actions to prevent neurotic suffering. It, like physical disorder, is likely to remain with us" (1988:64). And so, he concludes, "the critics are quite right in supposing that a fully satisfied human, with no failures, no sense of wrongdoing, no griefs, no fears, no longings for the eternal, would have no occasion to look for God. But it is they who are indulging in fantasy when they imagine such a creature and suppose it to be human" (1988:68).

Leavy wants to use psychoanalysis as a tool with which to think about religious experience, but he does not want to "adapt psychology to religion" (1988:74, slightly altered) and he is even more opposed to "preserving the intellectual respectability of religion by forcing it to submit to a secular language" (1988:80). Rather, Leavy prefers to keep the life of faith and the domain of science separate:

> All psychologies, to the extent that they make any scientific claim, stay within the realm of earthly experience to describe and try to explain the workings of the mind. Psychology cannot encompass the divine within its parameters. From the experience out of which I write, the two orders of existence—earthly and divine—are equally real and interactive; but we must be content in this life to keep them intellectually apart. (1988:74)

God and the world, faith and psychoanalysis, may interact but it is heuristically necessary to keep them distinct. (I have argued for such a dualism myself [1981] and traced the history of such a stance [1984].)

It is clear to me that though logically coherent such dualism serves an intellectually defensive function (see Jones 1984). It allows the religious person to keep his or her belief safe from scientific attack while also affirming the value of science. The two components of this dualistic solution to the relation between religion and science are (1) the insistence that science stick to its own domain and (2) the articulation of some reality essential to religion that lies outside the domain of science. Leavy's argument reflects both components.

One implication of such a dualistic position is that religion and psychoanalysis make sense only in the context of their own interpretive frameworks and particular constellations of experiences. "Religious faith within its own horizons," Leavy writes, "has its basis in a reality that is not confined by the subjectivity of the individual," which is the focal point of psychoanalysis (1988:81). And psychoanalysis "to the extent that [it] is a scientific understanding and not a disguised atheistic philosophy has no bearing on faith one way or another" (1986:152).

They must be kept separate so that the veracity of each domain is respected by the other. Leavy is concerned that when faith speaks in psychological categories the integrity of religion's claims are undercut and faith becomes "something equally accessible outside its domain . . . [becoming] 'metaphors' which are after all only a matter of taste" (1988:80). Lost is the intellectual authenticity of faith: "such modesty on the part of believers strikes me as uncalled for. It leaves out of account the prodigious claims of revealed religion and almost, if not quite, obliterates the testimony of religious experience" (1988:80).

Also lost is the transcendence of God. Although Leavy does not invoke that theological category, he clearly has such a notion in mind when he writes "the essence of the idea of God is that it—He/She—stands in opposition to culture, to the world" (1986:154). It is an inevitable loss, given that psychological categories are bound within the rim of finitude; they "stay within the realm of earthly experience" and so, by definition, are powerless to speak of transcendence at all. And thus the person of faith uses them at his or her peril.

In his reflections on common moments in human life, and especially the religiously informed life, Leavy demonstrates that psychoanalysis need not be antagonistic to the life of faith but rather can illuminate it. In his warning about reductionism (which infuses all his writing) and the dangers of the religious use of psychological categories, Leavy raises a core issue in the dialogue between religion and psychoanalysis: can the two disciplines respect each other's truth? Or must the psychoanalysis of religion be reductionistic and restrict religion to being a dependent variable? Or can the psychoanalysis of religion be conducted on a new basis on which the intellectual and spiritual integrity of religion can be preserved without recourse to the defense of dualism? I will return to these questions in the final chapter.

In Meissner, Rizzuto, and Leavy, then, we have three ways of moving beyond Freud's treatment of religion while remaining firmly grounded in psychoanalytic tradition. On the basis of both personal conviction and logical argument, these analysts see Freud's discussion of religion as one-sided and the differences between them come in part from the different post-Freudian psychoanalytic movements they draw upon in rethinking the psychoanalysis of religion: Leavy on Lacan, Meissner on Hartmann, and Rizzuto on Winnicott.

## Hans Loewald

Repeatedly I have noted Freud's continuing desire to understand the present in terms of the past. Parallel to this hermeneutic was a normative developmental theory advocating a linear progression from childishness to adulthood that defined mental health in direct proportion to how much the past had been outgrown. Freud's definition of maturity involved leaving the past behind while his interpretive approach implied the past could never be left behind.

In a series of lectures and writings, Hans Loewald complements Freud's model of understanding with a teleological hermeneutic of mental life in which dynamic processes are read forward as well as backward. His reflections provide another possibility for moving psychoanalysis beyond Freud's narrow interpretation of religion.

For Freud the id was the realm of blind self-centered instinctual chaos—the continuing potential for regression and neurosis within the individual. The best that could be hoped was to gain some rational control over it—"where id is, let ego be." Freud's was the Stoic's hope of rational self-mastery and resignation (for more on Freud's relation to Stoicism, see Rieff 1959). The worst fate was to fall prey to the blind irrational forces within.

In contrast, the id, for Loewald, is not simply a set of instincts to be controlled but also an energy to be tamed and transformed. Loewald uses Freud's term *sublimation* for the process by which basic instincts are rendered useful. But Freud's reductionistic undertow colored his understanding of sublimation so that all human activities were viewed as nothing but differing manifestations of a few basic instincts. As Loewald says, Freud's "view of sublimation always smacks of reduction. It also implies there is some element of sham or pretense in our greatly valued higher activities" (1978:75). For Freud, finally, instinct is never transformed, only controlled. For Loewald, real transformation of instinct is possible. Sublimation describes a process by which different spheres of mental activity are created while also remaining in contact with their primary source.

Both aspects of this dialectic are essential. Higher mental processes—what Freud called "secondary processes"—must be established out of our instinctual nature. But our "primary processes" must also remain available to us. Opposing Freud's attempt to keep id and ego, instinct and reason, in hermetically sealed compartments so that the purity of reason would not be contaminated by the irrationality of instinct, Loewald writes:

There is no one way street from id to ego. Not only do irrational forces overtake us again and again; in trying to lose them we would be lost. The id, the unconscious modes and contents of human experience, should remain available. If they are in danger of being unavailable—no matter what state of perfection our "intellect" may have reached—or if there is a danger of no longer responding to them . . . [we must find] a way back to them so they can be transformed, and away from a frozen ego. (1978:22)

This cycle of sublimation, moving out from instinct and back again, reveals that the id, the unconscious, is not simply the cause of neurosis. As the source of reason, it has a rationality all its own in which dichotomies are transcended and a unity apprehended:

If we acknowledge the undifferentiating unconscious as a genuine mode of mentation which underlies and unfolds into a secondary process mentation (and remains extant together with it, although concealed by it), then we regain a more comprehensive perspective—no doubt with its limitations yet unknown. Such a perspective betokens a new level of consciousness, of conscire, on which primary and secondary modes of mentation may be known together. (1978:64–65)

Another major characteristic of the knowing generated by the primary process—besides a sense of unity—is a sense of timelessness. In moments of aesthetic, sexual, or religious ecstasy, our ordinary linear sense of time is "overshadowed or pervaded by the timelessness of the unconscious or primary process" (1978:67). Or a vivid sound, sight, or smell may propel us backward in time until we are unexpectedly reliving an episode in a moment in which past and present collapse "in a *now* that is not distinguished as present from past" (1978:66). Such "transtemporal" experiences point to a way of knowing that is "structured or centered differently, that beginning and ending, temporal succession and simultaneity, are not a part [of such experiences]. They are transtemporal in their inner fabric" (1978:68).

Thus Loewald stands both Freud's hermeneutic and his developmental trajectory on their heads. Genuine movement forward is possible. Therefore developmental stages should be read not only backward in terms of how they recapitulate the past but also forward in terms of where they are going. Each human action both repeats the past and points forward to new developmental possibilities.

For example, in illustrating where genuine development is possible, Loewald writes that the transference represents "an imaginative reorganization and elaboration of the early, life-giving love experiences" as well as "a reiteration of the same, an automatic, driven reenactment of early relationships" (1978:48). As he describes it, sublimation is not only a "defense" but also "belongs to the area of ego development" (1988:33). And the process of therapy aims at more than just keeping the lid on eternal and unchanging drives:

> Our drives, our basic needs, in such transformation are not relinquished, nor are traumatic and distorting childhood experiences made conscious in order to be deplored or undone—even if that were possible. They are part of the stuff our lives are made of. What is possible is to engage in the task of actively reorganizing, reworking, transforming those early experiences which, painful as many of them have been, first gave meaning to our lives. (1978:22)

For Freud, the past—represented by the id—remains unchanged throughout life, continually reappearing in new guises. For Loewald, genuine transformation and reworking are possible. Present behavior should be interpreted both in terms of where it came from and in terms of what it might develop into in the future; it should be read with regard for the future as well as the past. (A more detailed discussion of models of transformation in psychoanalytic theory can be found in Fingarette [1963].)

On the other hand, "To be an adult . . . does not mean leaving the child in us behind" (1978:21–22). Our earliest mental state is not simply something to be renounced, if not outgrown (as Freud thought), but also something to be returned to time and time again. Such returns are sources of creativity and refreshment. Discursive reason alone renders human life sterile and flat. Conscious reason "limits and impoverishes" existence unless it has access to the more unitive and intuitive forms of knowing grounded in the unconscious. In words Freud could never have said, Loewald writes:

> The range and richness of human life is directly proportional to the mutual responsiveness between these various mental phases and levels. . . . While [rational thought is] a later development, it limits and impoverishes . . .

the perspective, understanding, and range of human action, feeling, and thought, unless it is brought back into coordination and communication with those modes of experience that remain their living source, and perhaps their ultimate destination. It is not a foregone conclusion that man's objectifying mentation is, or should be, an ultimate end rather than a component and intermediate phase. (1978:61)

Primary processes with their complementary forms of rationality should be accessible to even the most highly developed intellect. Sanity consists not in renouncing primary process but in remaining open without becoming swamped by it. Seeds of this argument can be found in Loewald's earlier papers, such as "Ego and Reality" (1949) and "On Motivation and Instinct Theory" (1971) where he suggests that infantile consciousness cannot be simply outgrown in the interests of achieving objectivity. (Both papers are in Loewald 1980.)

Loewald is thus an advocate of a far richer vision of human experience than that of Freud's—"a new level of consciousness, of conscire, on which primary and secondary modes of mentation may be known together" (1978:65; a similar point in relation to Loewald is made by Chodorow 1989).

In a careful exegesis of Freud's *Civilization and Its Discontents,* Loewald shows how religion (and art, as discussed in his 1988 book) becomes a primary carrier of this "return, on a higher level of organization, to the early magic of thought, gesture, word, image, emotion, fantasy, as they become united again with what in ordinary nonmagical experience they only reflect, recollect, represent or symbolize . . . a mourning of lost original oneness and a celebration of oneness regained" (1988:81).

Religion, then, can serve to keep us open to ways of knowing and being that are rooted in the primary process with its unitary and timeless sensibility:

If we are willing to admit that instinctual life and religious life both betoken forms of experience that underlie and go beyond conscious and personalized forms of mentation—beyond those forms of mental life, of ordering our world, on which we stake so much—then we may be at a point where psychoanalysis can begin to contribute in its own way to the understanding of religious experience, instead of ignoring or rejecting its genuine validity or treating it as a mark of human immaturity. (1978:73)

Like all forms of conscious mental life (or sublimation), religion and art differentiate themselves from the primary process. They are not simply raw expressions of the unconscious. But, unlike more abstract forms of conscious rationality, in religion and art "the experience of unity [with the primary process] is restored, or at least evoked, in the form of symbolic linkage" (1988:45). Thus such a theory of sublimation leads Loewald inevitably to a discussion of symbolism (1988, chap. 4).

But unlike Meissner who discusses symbols primarily in terms of their transitional blend of objectivity and subjectivity, for Loewald the importance of symbols lies in their ability to evoke the experience of the primary process in such a way that all differentiation is not lost. Symbols draw us into a psychic realm in which we experience our connection with the primary process—experiences characterized by timelessness and unity—but in such a way that we do not lose our capacity for secondary process, unlike the schizophrenic who is so engulfed in the unconscious that all conscious rationality ceases (1988, chap. 4).

Symbols then are purely the product neither of the unconscious (like a dream) nor of rational consciousness; rather they are influenced by both levels of the mind. This point clearly parallels Meissner's claim that symbols are a blend of objectivity and subjectivity and so leads Loewald, as it did Meissner, to a consideration of Winnicott. Loewald does not agree with Winnicott's (and by extrapolation, Meissner's) formulation of the problem in terms of a tension between objectivity and subjectivity.

Loewald rejects Winnicott's contention that the infant moves from subjectivity to objectivity, aided by transitional objects.

> The journey does not start from the subjective; it is a journey from a state prior to the differentiation of subjectivity and objectivity to a state when subjectivity and objectivity come into being. Transitional objects and phenomena are transitional not by virtue of being in transit from subjectivity to objectivity but in so far as they represent way stations from indeterminacy to determinacy or from the ineffable to the effable. (1988:72)

The infant's experience is not one of subjectivity; it exists before the differentiation of objectivity and subjectivity, self and other. It is, however, ineffable and beyond the power of speech to comprehend (1988:74).

The infantile state—which is before subjective and/or objective consciousness—points to a wider notion of subjectivity that embraces both. Our consciousness of ourselves (which we usually call subjectivity) and our consciousness of objects (which we usually call objectivity) are both states of consciousness. Objectivity does not mean a lack of human awareness but rather a particular form of human awareness, one focused on the "not self." In objectivity the contents of my awareness do not belong to me (they are objects in the world of space and time) but my *awareness* of them still belongs to me and is mine and is, in that sense, subjective. Objectivity is not opposed to "subjectivity" (understood as human awareness) but is rather one form of it. Thus the attempt (which was partially, at least, Freud's) to create an "objective" psychoanalysis is inevitably doomed, for psychoanalysis is in fact "in the forefront of efforts to break the hegemony of the modern scientific *natura naturata* interpretation of reality" (1988:79; this paragraph is my restatement of Loewald's argument on pages 78–89).

Although he casts his discussion as a response to Winnicott, Loewald does not apply his conception of a "wider" subjectivity to a reformulation of Winnicott's idea of transitional phenomena except to say that he "suspect[s] that Winnicott would not have disagreed with an interpretation of subjectivity in a wider and different sense, as outlined here" (1988:80). If, however, there is no linear movement from id to ego, from subjectivity to objectivity, but rather a reciprocal movement between them and if there is a "wider" subjectivity that embraces both what we call objectivity and subjectivity, then when we use terms like *objectivity, subjectivity,* and *transitional phenomena,* we are really referring to differing permutations of consciousness, different states of awareness. And, like the primary process, which is known to us only through some second-order symbols of it, we never encounter that awareness in itself but only in conjunction with our awareness of ourselves or others. The implication, which we have encountered before, is that when speaking of "transitional objects," we are really speaking of a "transitional" state of consciousness.

Thus Loewald desires to reformulate the primary process in more positive terms and to speak for "the general validity or importance in human life of the different spheres and forms of experience" (1978:71). This enables him to appreciate religion in ways that Freud—with his totally negative view of the primary process—never could. And it leads Loewald beyond Freud's analysis of religion in a manner very different from Meissner's use of Hartmann and Rizzuto's use of Winnicott. But we shall see that Loewald's advocacy of a variety of states of consciousness, including the experience of unity and timelessness, does dovetail with Winnicott's interests. And his treatment of symbolism in religion and art as essential routes back into the primary process parallels some of Bollas's concerns that will be discussed in the final chapter.

## D. W. Winnicott

As is clear from the foregoing survey, the work of D. W. Winnicott has been central to the post-Freudian rethinking of the psychoanalysis of religion. Whether one finds his ideas helpful (as do Meissner and Rizzuto) or is skeptical of them (as are Loewald and Leavy), Winnicott has become a powerful figure in this area. Particularly important has been his discussion of transitional phenomena, the main features of which I have already outlined in my discussions of Meissner and Rizzuto.

"In psychoanalytic writing and in the vast literature that has been influenced by Freud," Winnicott notes, "there can be found the tendency to dwell either on a person's life as it relates to objects or else on the inner life of the individual" (1971:105). And one can add that this applies not only to psychoanalysis but to all of modern culture, which has been dominated by a split between the public and private worlds (Jones 1982). Opposing this dichotomy of public and private, objective and subjective, Winnicott clearly sees that a

> third part of the life of a human being, a part that we cannot ignore, is an intermediate area of *experiencing*, to which inner reality and external life both contribute. It is an area that is not challenged because no claim is made on its behalf except that it shall exist as a resting-place for the individual engaged in the perpetual human task of keeping inner and outer reality separate yet interrelated. (1971:2)

Between inner and outer lies interaction. Neither the objective environment nor the isolated individual but rather the interaction between them defines this third domain, for it "is a product of the *experiences of the individual person* (baby, child, adolescent, adult) in the environment" (1971:107).

This intermediate area begins to form in the interactional space between the mother and the infant and "can be thought of as occupying a potential space. . . . its foundation is the baby's trust in the mother *experienced* over a long-enough period" (1971:110). Good-enough caretaking provides the infant with enough trust in life's dependability that development is not thwarted and the infant can venture beyond the perimeter of his or her private world. "The potential space happens only in relation to a feeling of confidence on the part of the baby, that is, confidence related to the dependability of the mother-figure or environmental factors, confidence being the evidence of dependability that is becoming introjected" (1971:100).

Here are clear echoes of the interpersonal and interactional model of personality developed in the preceding chapter in reference to Fairbairn, Kohut, and others. Winnicott's famous dictum that "there is no such thing as a baby" but only the parent-child dyad makes this explicit (see Winnicott 1965; Greenberg and Mitchell 1983, chap. 7). This third or intermediate area of psychological functioning is clearly *an interpersonal experience*—first in relation to the mother in which there is a "separation that is not a separation but a form of union" (1971:98) and later in relation to "the whole cultural field," for "the place where cultural experience is located is in the *potential space* between the individual and the environment (originally the object)" (1971:100). Offering a harbinger of a relational model of selfhood, Winnicott's writings not only point to a new psychoanalytic paradigm but also hint at a relational model of the origin of culture and social institutions (Flax 1990).

As discussed earlier, the infant's movement into the world of objects is facilitated by the use of a "transitional object" which, being "neither *inside* nor *outside*" (1971:41), occupies that intermediate psychological space. The child's experience with the transitional object is neither objective nor subjective but rather interactional, and thus it can carry for the infant the security of her first interpersonal experience (1971:4).

The child plays with her transitional objects, and thus play is an essential part of the transitional process. Playing stands at the interface of the physical world and the world of inner psychological process. As Winnicott says,

This area of playing is not inner psychic reality. It is outside the individual, but it is not the external world. . . . Into this play area the child gathers objects or phenomena from external reality and uses these in the service of some sample derived from inner or personal reality. . . . In playing, the child manipulates external phenomena in the service of the dream and invests chosen external phenomena with dream meaning and feeling. (1971:51)

Thus, as Meissner emphasizes, the transitional process combines subjectivity and objectivity by the inner use of external objects.

But there is another sense (which does not figure as much in the writings of Meissner and Rizzuto) in which the transitional process transcends the dichotomy between subjectivity and objectivity—it takes place in an psychological space that is neither totally inward nor totally outward. Thus when Winnicott says that transitional phenomena are "always on the theoretical line between the subjective and that which is objectively perceived" (1971:50), he is referring to two different aspects of the same process: (1) the use of objects in the outer world in the service of projects originating in the inner world and (2) the creation of an interpersonal psychological space that is between the inner and outer worlds. He brings these both together when he writes, "The thing about playing is always the precariousness of the interplay of personal psychic reality and the experience of control of actual objects. This is the precariousness of magic itself, magic that arises in intimacy, in a relationship that is found to be reliable" (1971:47).

In play, the child invests physical things with private meanings and does so in a psychological space resonating with the earliest experiences of intimacy. Even when the baby plays alone, he is still operating interpersonally; the very experience of play (even by oneself) carries echoes of those first interactions, for "the playground is a potential space between the mother and the baby or joining mother and baby" (1971:47). Thus Winnicott's is not primarily a theory about certain kinds of objects— teddy bears and blankets—but is rather a theory about certain kinds of interpersonal experiences (and I think it is the weakness of Meissner's and Rizzuto's use of Winnicott that they tend to treat it as a theory about certain kinds of objects).

Transitional objects carry a certain interpersonal reality and perform a certain developmental function. Both form that state of consciousness or psychological space for which (as I noted before) Winnicott uses Freud's term *illusion:*

> I am therefore studying the substance of *illusion,* that which is allowed to the infant, and which in adult life is inherent in art and religion, and yet becomes the hallmark of madness when an adult puts too powerful a claim on the credulity of others, forcing them to acknowledge a sharing of illusion that is not their own. We can share a respect for *illusory experience,* and if we wish we may collect together and form a group on the basis of the similarity of our illusory experiences. This is a natural root of grouping among human beings. (1971:3)

The infusion of meaning from the inner world into actions and objects in the public sphere and/or the expression of inner-generated truths by means of external physical and verbal forms describes not only children's play with teddy bears and empty boxes but also the creation of symphonies, sculptures, novels, and even scientific theories. As noted before, "Cultural experience [is] an extension of the idea of transitional phenomena and of play" (1971:99). So when transitional objects recede into the background, there remains the residue of the creativity that drives the arts and the curiosity that drives the sciences—that is, the capacity to create culture. In an oft-quoted and moving passage about the fate of a transitional object, Winnicott writes,

> Its fate is to be gradually allowed to be decathected, so that in the course of years it becomes not so much forgotten as relegated to limbo. By this I mean that in health the transitional object does not "go inside" nor does the feeling about it necessarily undergo repression. It is not forgotten and it is not mourned. It loses meaning, and this is because the transitional phenomena have become diffused, have become spread out over the whole intermediate territory between "inner psychic reality" and "the external world as perceived by two persons in common," that is to say, over the whole cultural field. At this point my subject widens out into that of play, and of artistic creativity and appreciation, and of religious feeling, and of dreaming. (1971:5)

In discussing transitional objects, Winnicott is not just talking about "child's play" but proposing nothing less than a psychoanalytic theory of culture that begins from the interpersonal matrix of infant and parent, moves to the development of creativity through play and the use of transitional objects, and ends with the symphonies of Beethoven, the paintings of Rembrandt, and the theories of Einstein. "For cultural experience, including its most sophisticated developments, the position is the *potential space* between the baby and the mother" (1971:107), and "cultural experiences are in direct continuity with play, the play of those who have not yet heard of games" (1971:100).

Although transitional objects fade into the background, the need that gave rise to them remains. Having moved from the world of pure subjectivity into a less responsive external world, the self is forever caught in the tension of inner and outer and the struggle to relate his or her personal longings and insights to the "not-me world of objects." Thus the desire to integrate or transcend the dichotomy of inner and outer, subjective and objective, lives on long after the teddy bear has been forgotten. "The task of reality-acceptance is never completed," Winnicott writes. "No human being is free from the strain of relating inner and outer reality, and that relief from this strain is provided by an intermediate area of experience which is not challenged (arts, religion, etc.). This intermediate area is in direct continuity with the play area of the small child who is 'lost' in play" (1971:13).

Ultimately what is involved in the transitional process is the creation of "an intermediate area of *experience*," a psychological space resonant with the interpersonal world of infancy, out of which creativity emerges and in which the tension between objectivity and subjectivity is at least temporarily overcome and inner and outer worlds momentarily fuse. Summarizing his disparate thoughts on this subject, Winnicott writes,

> I have tried to draw attention to the importance both in theory and in practice of a third area, that of play, which expands into creative living and into the whole cultural life of man. This third area has been contrasted with inner or personal psychic reality and with the actual world in which the individual lives, which can be objectively perceived. I have located this important area of *experience* in the potential space between the individual and the environment. . . . it is here that the individual experiences creative living. (1971:102–103)

In his drive to go beyond the dualism of objectivity and subjectivity, Winnicott carries into psychoanalysis a theme that has dominated much current philosophy of science (Jones 1981; Bernstein 1983) as well as other contemporary movements. His search for "the intermediate area between the subjective and that which is objectively perceived" (1971:3) is clearly part of a larger cultural concern (Jones 1982).

The transitional process involves three components that stand in different ways at the intersection of objectivity and subjectivity: (1) a state of consciousness fashioned in an interpersonal matrix encompassing inner and outer worlds, (2) an external object used in the service of internal states, and (3) the external object functioning to facilitate moving from the world of subjectivity to the world of objects (and back again). In Meissner and Rizzuto we have seen different ways of applying this schema to the psychoanalytic understanding of religion: Meissner envisions religious forms as transitional *objects;* Rizzuto defends the importance of imagination and play.

Leavy is critical of the theological appropriation of Winnicott because he is afraid that it reduces religion to the status of a teddy bear to be used in the service of our mental health (1986:155). Loewald is critical of this use of Winnicott not only because he understands the infantile state differently but also because of the pejorative meaning of the term *illusion* (1988:66–82). But both Winnicott and Loewald reframe realities that Freud was suspicious of—Winnicott with illusion and Loewald with primary process—in the service of an appreciation of a variety of states of consciousness beyond the sensory-empirical mode that dominated Freud and positivistic science.

There is also an aspect of the transitional process to which Meissner and Rizzuto pay less attention—the creation of a special realm of experience—and in the last chapter I will return to the implications of this dimension of the transitional process for religion.

### Toward a New Psychoanalysis of Religion

The newer models of transference, surveyed in the first chapter, contain a theory of selfhood and psychopathology that takes the student of religion in a rather different direction from those just described. These models speak less of pathological individuals and more of neurotic interconnections. (This suggestion illustrates another congruence between self psychology and general systems theory.) For example, implicit in Kohut's theory is the principle that our sense of self is but one pole of an interaction: a cohesive and vigorous self is one side of a mirroring and affirming dyad. On the other hand, a neurotic self is one pole of a deformed and deforming relationship: a sense of self as humiliated and guilty requires a critical and judgmental selfobject bond. A confident and buoyant self reflects approving others, whereas a self that feels diminished and weak points to a distant and uninvolved selfobject. In all these cases, the self we are is but one pole of the relationships through which we sustain ourselves.

Such models of transferential understanding would shift the focus of the psychoanalytic study of religion. Congruent with this model of analytic understanding, religion would be defined not primarily as a defense against instincts or a manifestation of internalized objects but rather as a *relationship* (with God, the sacred, the cosmos, or some reality beyond the phenomenal world of space and time). And the psychoanalytic study of religion would investigate the way in which individuals' religious beliefs, experiences, and practices reflect the dynamics active in their construing of experience and in the deep structure of their internalized relationships.

Thus the origin of religion would be found not in the need to ward off the return of the repressed nor in the process of consolidating internal object representations but in the necessity for every cohesive and energetic self to exist in a matrix of relationships. Every child (except in cases of severe psychopathology) is developing a sense of self. It is primarily this core sense of who we are, rather than an instinctual conflict, that is acted out in the transference. For this core sense of who we are is intimately connected to the way in which we construe our experience and our fundamental patterns of interaction. Just as, according to Rizzuto, the idea of God is developmentally necessary to ground our earliest awareness of the existence of things, perhaps a God is needed also to ground our sense of who we are: the child who feels secure grounds that security in a caring God; the child who feels guilty and terrible grounds that sense of self by reference to a wrathful God; the child who feels estranged envisions a distant deity or dreams of a compensatory, warm, and tender selfobject God.

This last point can be illustrated by a striking historical example. The eighteenth century, the Age of Reason—when the Newtonian world picture with its cold dead universe and implication that we are strangers in it was becoming widespread—produced two religious movements, deism, the religion of the distant father and the cold cosmos, and Methodism, the religion of the warm and tender Jesus.

The dynamics of selfhood are the dynamics of interconnection. And all the self's activities—the goals it pursues or renounces, the intimacies it establishes or flees from, the gods it worships or denies, and the patterns that echo and reecho through those activities—all reflect the deep structure of the relational self.

Rizzuto suggests much the same thing in proposing a "dialectical" (or dialogical) view of selfhood. But she does not expand it into a coherent model of religion and her relational language tends to get submerged in her more extensive use of the terminology of the British object relations school.

Kohut, too, suggests that God may function as one pole of a selfobject bond and that the capacity to "create substitute selfobjects via visual imagery when external reality is devoid of tangible selfobjects must be counted among newly acquired assets" in a successful analysis (1984:76). This, Kohut acknowledges, leads to a "nonapologetically positive assessment of the role and significance of art and religion . . . which differs from the assessment of classical analysis" (1984:76). But he, too, did not elaborate this insight into a more detailed theory of religion. Both Rizzuto and Kohut imply that God or the God representation might serve to ground the sense of self, but neither conducts an in-depth analysis of religious phenomena along these lines.

The task of this book is to explore the ways in which a person's relationship with what he construes as sacred or ultimate serves as the transferential ground of the self. Freud understood transference and therefore religion in terms of the category of projection. But such a metaphor depends on an essentially atomistic worldview where one isolated being projects something essentially private and subjective onto a separate object. Rather, following Kohut's maxim that a self never exists outside of a selfobject milieu, our central term *transferential ground* refers to a *relationship* and our focus will be on the person's relationship—her affective bond—with what is sacred in her life. We will focus primarily not on doctrinal belief or ritual participation but on *the affective bond with the sacred.* Rather than defense mechanisms or God objects (transitional or otherwise), this phrase, "the affective bond with the sacred," captures the focal point for a new psychoanalysis of religion.

Such a study of religion would involve the investigation of three related questions. First, the emphasis would not be on understanding religion primarily through the category of the God image, as object relations investigators (such as Rizzuto) have often done. Rather the focus here would be on analyzing how religion as a *relationship* resonates to those internalized relationships that constitute the sense of self—or, to put it slightly differently, how a relationship to the sacred enacts and reenacts the transferential patterns present throughout a person's life. For the images about which Rizzuto writes are not simply neutral pictures, they are the bearers of intense, affectively charged relationships. Thus any study of the psychological origin of the God image should be complemented by a study of the psychological origins of the God relationship and how that relationship is constellated out of the internalized relationships that make up the self.

This would entail starting with these various internalized relationships and investigating psychologically how an individual's relationship with his God is made from them. One might explore what projective identifications are at work in the person's relationship with his God. Does the deity carry an internalized critical parent imago so that coming into the presence of God re-creates that relationship of fear and judgment? Or does God function to sustain self-cohesion as the perfectly mirroring selfobject? Or does that sense of being one of the favored offspring of the supreme being mobilize a broken grandiose self? Is a detached selfobject matrix re-created through investing the self in intellectualizing about an abstract world spirit or universal system of energy? Is a relationship to a chronically unavailable primary caretaker continued through a perpetually unresolved search for the meaning of life? Is a warm symbiotic bond re-created, or the lack of it compensated for, through the intimacies of a baptism in the Holy Spirit or a merger with the Great Mother or the vast ocean of being? What inner relational patterns go into our devotional exercises, meditational disciplines, philosophical theologies?

Second, since transference is the person's most fundamental pattern of interaction and meaning-making, it makes sense that in relation to God (as the repository of what is most fundamentally valuable or important to a person) these transferential patterns and associated attitudes and affects would appear most clearly. Thus a second line of psychological investigation would be the study of how a person's relationship to what she considers sacred discloses these primary transferential patterns in her life. From a person's vision of God and the affective tone of the bond to her God, something of her sense of self might be inferred. This line of investigation is the reverse of the previous one and would involve starting with a person's descriptions of her relationship to her God and using this description as a vehicle for gaining insight into her larger relational world.

What relationships within the inner object world are made conscious by the language of the sacred as void and abyss and the image of the self forever vanishing in the ocean of being? What organizing themes are disclosed by seeing the Virgin Mary floating on a cloud, or hearing "the sound of one hand clapping," or knowing that "the ways of Tao are effortless." What introjected relationships are reenacted by being "a sinner in the hands of an angry God," by "walking alone in the garden with Jesus," by "resting in the arms of the Great Mother," by "being grasped by the ground of being," by realizing that "God does not play dice," by resigning oneself to fate, or by "experiencing the state of no-mind?" What inner relational patterns resonate in the koans of Zen Buddhism, the syntheses of Aquinas and Barth, the tragedies of Homer, and the speculations of the Upanishads?

A third question, an aspect of the second, would study the connection between the coming of a new sense of self and the development of a new image of God. This would involve tracing the changes in a person's sense of self and his transferential patterns and seeing how these changes mirrored and were mirrored in his relationship to his God. An example of this kind of analysis in the Kohutian framework can be found in the recent study of the occult by Gay (1989), in which he argues that occult and other paranormal experiences happen after a significant selfobject loss.

Learning psychoanalysis is more than mastering a body of theory. It also involves learning to listen in a certain way: to hear new themes and find different connections between apparently discrete fragments of dreams, behaviors, fantasies, and feelings. Embracing a relational model of personality is more than learning another set of terms; it entails listening for echoes of past interpersonal patterns and their affective tones in present relationships, including the relationship with the sacred.

Thus a new psychoanalytic investigation of religion concerns more than finding examples of psychoanalytic concepts (oedipal complexes or bad objects) in religious texts and proclamations. It requires listening for those internalized interpersonal themes reverberating still in present religious experiences, involves acquiring a fairly detailed knowledge of the subject's psychodynamics and so can probably be done only in the context of the clinical case study. This chapter has outlined what current models of transference might contribute to the psychoanalytic study of religion to provide a theoretical rationale for such a project. The next chapter will present four case studies in which we will listen for some inner relational melodies.

CHAPTER

# 3

TRANSFERENCE

AND THE

DYNAMICS OF RELIGION

The focus of this chapter will be primarily on the function of the God image in the person's psychic economy rather than on its origin. The category of transference is the major lens through which I will address this question of function. Clearly this shift in emphasis from origin to function mirrors the shift in the understanding of the transference that has taken place in modern psychoanalytic theorizing.

If it is the case, as previously suggested, that religion can be conceptualized as a form of transference in the interpersonal sense described in the first chapter, then there ought to be parallels between the transferential patterns occurring in many places in a person's life, especially as it develops in therapy, and that person's affective bond with the sacred. This chapter will investigate and illustrate that possibility.

There are any number of ways one might investigate such a question. For example, I tried a pilot project in which people filled out open-ended questionnaires about their images of God and their feelings about God. The procedure provided a tremendous diversity of data from seemingly vague concepts of God and amorphous feelings of relationship toward God to concrete and specific descriptions of the deity and evocative recitations of immediate religious experiences. But though this method garnered a wide sample of data, it seemed too static for my purposes and could not capture the transformations of religious experience.

So instead I pursued my inquiry in a way that is much narrower but also runs deeper and more readily captures the vicissitudes of people's religion: the case study. Although perhaps not broad enough to yield generalizable results, case studies may be deep enough to yield provocative questions. The central category of understanding in this study is transference. The investigation of transference and of religion as a form of transference involves process, and to examine process, the most effective way would seem to be the case study.

I shall briefly describe four clinical cases and draw connections between the vicissitudes of the transference as it emerged in therapy and the dynamics of religion in each person's life. These cases were rewritten to disguise the patient's identities. Clinical encounters are reported verbatim, but identifying information has been radically altered.

### *Harold*

Harold is a forty-one-year-old businessman, Protestant all his life, who consulted me originally because of an inability to get on with his life after a bitter marital breakup and chronic divorce litigation. He had been married fifteen years to a domineering woman who controlled every aspect of his life and finally left him for another man. She then hired an aggressive lawyer and got a highly favorable settlement (including sole custody of their two sons) because Harold refused to fight her.

His parents had lived together in a distant relationship. His father, who was probably alcoholic, spent long hours at work, which his mother endured with stoical resignation and a whiff of moral superiority. She was very critical of Harold who probably served as a stand-in for his frequently absent father. His younger sister fared better in terms of the mother's anger. The atmosphere around the house was that men were untrustworthy and irresponsible. Harold took upon himself the task of changing his mother's mind about men; he made the honor roll, worked an after-school job, put himself through college, found a position in a large bank, got married, and produced grandchildren—all to no avail.

A hard and conscientious worker, his basic stance in life was one of extreme passivity. Passed over for promotion several times, he remained at an intermediate job level rather than confront his supervisors. His wife organized his life down to the smallest details of his dress, his reading, his friends, and his relationship with their sons.

This pattern of passivity was also played out in the transference. His never-ending efforts to get me to tell him what to do and my continual refusal produced a constant struggle between us. "I need direction," he would insist. "I need a kick in the butt to get going." He brought crisis after crisis in the long divorce process into therapy in the hopes that I would advise him on how to handle them. Or he would wait passively in the sessions for me to set the agenda. The pattern was clear: he would get angry at people when they didn't tell him what to do, but he would become resentful and passively aggressive when they did. I worked as hard as I could to avoid the trap.

The turning point in therapy came when he finally became openly angry at me for not telling him what to do. He then expected me to criticize him for his rage. My accepting and understanding it and refusing to be diverted by it enabled him to get past the anger and see the pattern of passivity operating in his life. Gradually he became less passive, standing up for himself at work, changing jobs, and refusing to settle for the lopsided divorce agreement.

The change was reflected in his understanding of God. Part of what kept him so passive was his highly critical superego, always telling him he was wrong and making a mistake. Afraid to take risks, he had to be a pleaser. His idea of God served to carry this superego function. God was someone keeping score on him, always needing to be pleased, ready to find the least mistake. His relationship with God was tinged with fear, anxiety, and anger. Thus God was assimilated into the role in his psychic economy also filled by his mother and wife. And he responded to his God in a similar way: passively, half-compliantly, which only exacerbated his guilt.

The course of the transference was mirrored by a transformation in his religious life. At the end of treatment, I asked him about any changes in his image of God (as I ask all my patients for whom religion is important), and he responded that the biggest change he noticed was in the area of prayer. "I don't expect God to do everything for me anymore," he told me. "I used to expect God to tell me what to do. Now I know I have to do more than listen, I have to *do* something too." A sentence that could stand as a summary of the whole course of treatment.

Rather than being dominated by the presence of a judgmental dictator, his faith now contained themes of his taking personal responsibility, being a steward of what God had given him, learning more about his religion so that he was not so dependent on others to tell him what was right and wrong. For example, he started a study group on business ethics in his church; he took the initiative to convince the pastor of the need for it and organized and publicized it. In the area of his faith, as in the other areas of his life, he took a more active role. The image of a God who desired only passive compliance had to change to fit the new experience of himself in therapy and the other areas of his life.

### Sylvia

Sylvia, age twenty-seven, works as a secretary. Raised in a Pentecostal church, she recently joined a mainline Protestant denomination. She was born in Eastern Europe. Her family immigrated to the United States when she was five and settled in an Eastern European Pentecostal ghetto. Her parents still could speak no English when they died, after twenty years in America. They were suspicious of others and trusted only members of their subculture. Thus there was a strong boundary around her community and few boundaries within it. Partly as a result of that, she had suffered a long history of childhood sexual abuse and incest.

Sylvia carried the secret of that abuse with her, afraid to tell anyone. Once she had tried to speak to her mother, but her mother washed her mouth out with soap because what she was saying was "dirty." As a result of her secret, she felt different from others and drew into herself, growing more and more isolated. Given their strong emphasis on community and belonging, the people around her began to shun Sylvia in response to her withdrawal. Finally she left the ghetto and moved in with a high school friend who got Sylvia a job where she worked. It was years before members of her family spoke to her again.

The major struggle in therapy was over acceptance. Exceptionally intelligent, although not well educated, Sylvia quickly grasped the impact the forces that governed her early life had had upon her: the isolation and suspicion of the community, her fear of being discovered, the aloofness of her family, the guilt and anger that colored her earliest years. Therapy provided a safe place where these stormy emotions could be understood and accepted.

Sylvia's own words best describe the core of our therapeutic relationship. During termination, when asked what had been most important in her therapy, she said:

> For hours and hours you struggled with me, fighting with me, battling my defenses against your acceptance. Finally I had to say to myself, you must care or you wouldn't fight so hard. Fighting you made me realize how I repel others' acceptance. You kept questioning that. Finally you got me to question why I did that. That was the biggest change in therapy; now I accept others' care and compliments.
>
> In getting past the abuse, you were patient with me, you didn't push me to face it too fast. That made me see, if someone really cared, they would be patient with me, too. It's okay to ask someone to understand and be patient.
>
> The most helpful thing in therapy was the experience of having someone hanging in there with me, of caring enough to stick with me. That made it possible to understand myself, seeing that I could be understood. I realized I could do that for myself too. I could understand and accept what had happened to me because you understood and accepted what happened.

Sylvia's early view of herself mirrored her sense of isolation. She felt there was something terribly wrong with her, that she was different and incomprehensible. Her experience of being understood and accepted, when she finally let it into her consciousness, forced a change in that sense of self. This, in turn, forced a change in her view of God. Again, in her own words:

> God is no longer a judge. I used to prefer judgmental religion; now I feel it does harm, it's not good. I see God as more forgiving. I see parts of Scripture about God's love that I never saw before.

An aloof, impatient God (reflecting her family) made sense of her experience when she was feeling isolated and maladjusted. But it could no longer give meaning to her experience of herself when she became more empathic and accepting.

Just as in the transference, patience has become a major category in her relationship with God. "I see," Sylvia said, "that God's love is greater than my mistakes." Her view of God as more patient and accepting is clearly connected to her therapeutic experience of patience and acceptance and her newfound capacity to be patient with herself. But was there a more causal connection, at least in her experience?

"Did God's love help you to accept yourself with your mistakes and guilt?" I asked her.

"No," she said, "it was the other way around. Only after I accepted myself could I accept that God and others cared."

The same process went on in her religious life as in the transference. At first, she fought against my acceptance, keeping me at a distance. She did the same with her God. "I always thought of God as loving; I always knew God was guarding me, yet didn't really feel it or experience it," she said of her early religious life. In the course of therapy, she gradually stopped fighting the therapist's empathy, accepting it and turning it toward herself. Exactly the same process occurred in her religious life. Again, in Sylvia's words:

> At first when I would pray to God, I would hear God address me simply as "my child." Later, as "my little child." And now I hear God call me "my little wounded child."

Her experience of God as one who could accept her woundedness parallels her own acceptance of that woundedness.

### Barbara

Barbara, age thirty-five, comes from an evangelical Protestant background. She has a master's degree in social work and is a social worker in a group home for women addicts. She has a history of early adolescent sexual abuse and incest by an older brother. Barbara was the youngest of three children who were deserted by their father when she was an infant. Her mother, totally unskilled, was left with the sole responsibility for them, a task that consumed all her energy. Her oldest brother also worked after school, so she was left in the care of her other brother, who resented it and was inclined to take out his frustrations on his sister.

In her middle twenties, Barbara married a man she met in graduate school. Her relationship with her husband (who has since left the field of social work to go into business) was described as good. They had no children because she doubted her ability to be a good mother. She came to therapy because of depression and recurring suicidal thoughts. She felt overworked and taken advantage of on her job but was unable to act to change the situation. Her irresolution over having children was also a sticking point. Her husband had been patient with her fears but he wanted children, and her indecision was threatening the marriage. I saw her for three years, during which time her depression lifted and her self-confidence improved enough for her to change jobs and become pregnant.

During the termination phase of therapy I asked Barbara how therapy had affected her view of God and her religious life. Her response was so striking that I am going to use it as the organizational format for presenting her case. Over the new two weeks she came with extensive notes describing three different images of God, each one representing a different stage of her life.

*1. Childhood God Representation.* Her childhood image of God, she said, had been God the judge, keeping records on everybody. She described an image in her mind right out of Cecil B. deMille: God was an old man with a beard and a record book.

"During those years," she said, "I saw myself as worthless. I felt so guilty because of what my brother and I were doing." This critical God supported her sense of worthlessness, born of being abused. God was simply another man who abused her. Not from a religious family, Barbara during early adolescence joined an evangelical Protestant community church. This was about the same time as the sexual abuse began. This church was dealing with the same issues of guilt and forgiveness that were troubling her, but not in a way that was helpful. The pastor, she reported, spent more time talking about guilt than forgiveness, and the church's teaching made forgiveness contingent on moral perfection, which was obviously beyond her, given among other things the incestuous relationship. So that particular theology of forgiveness served only to reinforce her feelings of guilt. And the wrathful deity fit in well with her guilty and condemning conscience, serving to reinforce the

conscience and the feelings of worthlessness that tinctured every relationship, including her relationship with God. The God she found there
was what she imagined all along God would be like. As Rizzuto says,
"No child arrives at the 'house of God' without his pet God under his
arm" (1979:8).

2. *Young-Adult God Representation.* In her twenties, Barbara reported,
her image of God shifted to God the friend and Jesus the companion.
These were the years when she completed her professional education,
married, and found a job, achievements that enabled her to feel better
about herself. This new image of God served to bolster and express her
newfound sense of connection—with her husband, clients, coworkers,
and eventually a therapist. She entered therapy in her early thirties at the
close of this period of settling down because the changes she had hoped
would alleviate her chronic depression had failed to do so.

3. *Current God Representation.* At the time of termination, in her middle
thirties, she told me that she couldn't describe in words her current
image of God. But she came to the next session with a beautiful free-
form sculpture, part of which she had painted in vibrant colors so that it
resembled an abstract form of flowers and leaves. She could not describe
God, but she could represent God with images of growth and life. Here
she had portrayed an energy or force that was at once an abstract but also
intimate image of God, "in whom," she said, quoting the New Testa-
ment, "we live and move and have our being." This image of God served
to express and sustain her newfound will to experiment, change, and
grow. Besides changing jobs and entering parenthood, Barbara at termination was taking sculpture lessons, along with t'ai chi and aerobics.

When asked about the most important factors in her therapy, Barbara
said, "Your acceptance of me made the difference. I finally understood
that you really were there. I realized you were there even when I fought
to keep you out. This was a great comfort to me." This experience of
sustained comfort and support was reflected in her latest image of a God
who is always there—an abiding life energy, universal but also intimately personal.

Again, changes taking place in the transference and the transformations in her sense of self forced a reworking of her image of God. As Barbara said, in words that could stand as a summary of this chapter, "I couldn't think of myself as acceptable and still think of God as condemning."

## Martin

Martin is a thirty-nine-year-old associate professor of English who originally consulted me because of a writer's block. He had written a brilliant thesis at Harvard on the nature of literary criticism that was immediately published and that, along with a few articles and reviews, earned him tenure at a large university. When he consulted me, he had been working for three years on a second book, but new ideas eluded him and words ceased to flow. He came to me wondering if hypnosis would help him resolve the problem quickly (I had recently treated a friend of his for public-speaking phobia with a few sessions of hypnosis).

It soon became clear that more than a few sessions of hypnosis would be required. He was virtually without affect or animation, even when talking about Jewish novelists of the twentieth century—his favorite subject and the topic of a popular graduate seminar and the stillborn book. Apparently the enthusiasm of his students motivated him in the classroom, but when faced with a typewriter or my direct questions, his mind went blank.

Martin's father was a physician; his mother, a high school science teacher and principal. They had met in college, married in their senior year, and supported each other through years of graduate school. Martin's account portrayed two parents deeply involved in their work and each other but less so with Martin and his younger sister. It was a family in which books were read and discussed and ideas considered the most valuable part of life. Martin and his sister were never pressured to achieve in school. But partly because of the head start provided by an intellectually stimulating family and partly because their parents' values were so clear they never needed articulating, both children left high school as class valedictorians and went on to prestigious colleges. At first Martin wanted to be a journalist and writer, but the family commitment to graduate education and scholarship prevailed and he became an English professor instead.

In graduate school he had met a struggling poet. Vivacious and energetic, but a little unfocused, Jennifer welcomed Martin's interest in her work and his help with her career. He thrived on her warmth and liveliness, and the two had married in less than a year. Now she spent her days writing at home and sometimes assisting with courses at the university. Although Martin tended to withdraw from her, she deeply appreciated the structure and support he brought into her life and remained loyal to him. She was the one person who could always cheer him up.

The focus of therapy soon shifted from his blocked writing to the feelings of emptiness that threatened to swallow him whenever he sat down to write. If others brought energy to him, he could respond, but left on his own, he was unable to act.

Exploring that engulfing black tide reconnected Martin with the aloof and competitive atmosphere in which he grew up and eventually to the rage born of emotional neglect. It was actually not a vacuum at all but one side of a dike holding back a cascading fury. As a child Martin dealt with his fury, as his father and mother had theirs, by a tight control that generalized from the anger to squeeze out all emotion; he also relieved some of his fury intellectually through understated but vicious criticism of others' ideas. Such cognitive aggression served Martin well in his climb up the academic hierarchy from brilliant undergraduate to impressive graduate student to respected professor. The language in which he described his scholarship was clearly the language of aggression: he spoke of "attacking" a problem, "tearing apart a poem or novel," and "conquering" those who disagreed with him; he most liked to describe himself as a "critic." He had also learned to elicit small amounts of his parents' attention by doing well and fulfilling their expectations.

In graduate school the stimulus of attacking others' theories and the steady admiration of his teachers drove Martin to achieve. Now, on his own, those motivations gradually lost their power. In the inner ring of his profession, there were few parental surrogates left to impress or whose approval still needed winning. He realized also that now he had to produce a creative statement of his own and not just live as a parasitical critic of others' positions. But having cut himself off from his inner resources in an attempt to control his rage and model himself on his parents, he had nothing to draw on.

In the course of therapy, we finally gained access to the buried rage. As his anger began to flow, I encouraged him to spend an hour a day at his typewriter, pounding whatever angry words came to mind onto the page. For weeks he came to therapy with reams (or so it seemed) of pages filled with angry words, phrases, vignettes from his past. But gradually the words changed from outpourings of fury to thoughts about modern literature. And he also began to notice themes he had overlooked in the novels he was analyzing. Treatment stopped when the final draft of a four-hundred-page manuscript was on its way to a university press.

Martin was not a religious man. His parents had refused to celebrate Hanukkah or Christmas, saying that they didn't believe in religion and gave their kids plenty of gifts throughout the year. At termination I asked him how his outlook on life had changed in the course of therapy, and he began to talk spontaneously about metaphysics and his view of reality.

In high school and college, religion had functioned for him, as it had for his parents, as the target of his most sarcastic wit and as something on which to blame all the ills of humankind. Also like his parents, he prided himself on living by rationality alone. Although he was not a scientist, his view of reality (by which he meant the physical world) mirrored that of Newtonian science; the universe was cold, dead, impersonal. His worldview also mirrored the impersonal, unresponsive milieu in which he had grown up, and it formed the basis of his approach to literature. He once told me,

> That's what the novels of the twentieth century are about. How to find meaning in a meaningless space. How we dodge that awful truth, that there's no reason to live and yet we must find a reason to live. Are we cowards or heroes that we don't give up but go on living? That's the question behind modern fiction. They don't answer the question, they don't even discuss it directly. That's for philosophers, to waste their time spinning their wheels. Novelists simply chronicle the billions of ways we have of ignoring reality.

At the same time, his life was dominated by a search for truth. The ideal of truth carried the aura of the sacred for Martin: it was his overriding concern and major motivation; searching for it gave meaning to life and attaining it was a goal worthy of a lifetime. The search for truth, like the quest for the Holy Grail, assumed a virtually mythic position in his life and that of his family. But truth always seemed to elude his grasp. Unlike the relatively concrete problems of diagnosis his father worked at solving, understanding the meaning of a novel seemed an endless search. He could never reach it; the truth of the novel and of the process of the novelist's craft always escaped him.

His relationship to his own work and to the ideal of truth was Sisyphean. Truth itself became a black hole threatening to swallow him. In the three years before he came to see me, he drove himself harder and harder, trying to obtain the unobtainable and getting nowhere.

The dynamic between distance and intimacy formed the core of the transference. Martin kept me at bay by withholding his feelings and not revealing the guts of his life. When empathy and understanding began to draw him into the therapeutic relationship, he distanced himself with anger and sarcasm. But my willingness to withstand and accept (and even encourage) his anger kept the relationship going.

As the relationship deepened, another dynamic appeared. Instead of withholding himself from me, he began to accuse *me* of holding back on *him*. He insisted I tell him my response to his every comment, and when I didn't, he attacked me for withholding the truth of his life from him. A turning point in therapy came with the realization of the symmetry in what was happening in his therapy (I was withholding the truth from him), how he felt about his work (the final truth about literature was being withheld from him), and how he felt growing up (his parents withheld themselves from him). This insight made clear the parallel between his search for a final truth and his search for a relation to his parents; both were frantic but futile efforts.

Under the impact of the therapeutic relationship, his slightly paranoid view of reality as cold and impersonal, something hiding its secrets from him, gradually changed. His scholarly quest no longer had to carry his search to discover some ideal but hidden relationship, nor did it have to serve as an outlet for his anger and frustration.

In keeping with his intellectual nature, Martin at the end described the change in him brought about by therapy in primarily cognitive terms:

My view of the world changed. The physical universe may still be hard and solid but reality is essentially neutral. It's not hiding something from me, challenging me to discover the truth of human nature through its expression in the work of novelists and poets. It's just there, neutral, blank. The physical universe may be indifferent to me, but life contains creativity and ecstasy as well as that physical indifference. Different writers capture different aspects of reality. And different critics, like myself, find or create even further meanings from these works. But now I'm content to work along at it; I don't have to find the answer in capital letters.

Although he did not cast his description in religious terms, clearly Martin's fundamental sense of himself and reality and his relation to reality changed in therapy. A cold, impersonal, withholding world had given way to a richer and more complex metaphysics. And there was a parallel between the changes that took place transferentially and those that occurred metaphysically: he had shifted from feeling distanced and shut out to appreciating mystery and complexity:

It's just a mystery. Here's this universe of cold atoms and out of it comes, of all things, poems and novels. From a totally predictable world of unfailing forces and laws comes the totally unexpected—symphonies, sculptures, verse, and parable. It's supposed to be natural selection and survival of the fittest, yet we choose to use our time to put words onto pages and new sounds into the air. What survival value can that have? Yet it makes us human.

The militant atheism underlying his early vision of literature was transferentially grounded, a projection of his cold and impersonal parent-child experience onto the cosmos, re-creating a milieu in which he could continue the doomed struggle to wrest something from an unresponsive matrix. At the end of therapy it had given way to a more open and nuanced vision of the mystery of life as expressed through art, reflecting a richer and more complex way of relating to the world around him.

## A Note on Images of a Judgmental God

The three cases of people raised in religious families represented a movement from God as judge to God as source of love and forgiveness. Although no wider generalization can be drawn from the three cases, such a shift in God image does parallel the course of the transference in the successful treatment of many neurotics who, religious or not, come to therapy burdened with guilt and self-condemnation and leave more self-accepting.

There are several possible explanations for the apparent prevalence of this judgmental image of God in childhood.

1. An obvious cultural reason for such an image of God in childhood is that many parents use God as a means of social control, which is then internalized and serves as the basis for the child's image of God.

2. Freud's theory suggests that the superego develops in childhood out of an intrapsychic need to control the instincts and to internalize the father's and society's prohibitions. God is then the projection of this controlling superego. Superegos inherently tend to be harsh because of the contravailing instinctual power. They are more apt to shout "No, never" than to say gently "Yes, sometimes."

3. Rizzuto's suggestion that the image of God is built out of parental images helps make sense of this clinical material. But though one main parenting function in early childhood is disciplining the child, another, equally important, function is nurturing the child. Why does that function often figure less powerfully in constructing an image of God? Is it simply that people with more nurturing parents produce more nurturing images of God and vice versa? Research does not suggest such a simple correlation between parental images and God images (Spilka et al., 1964, 1975; Vergote and Aubert 1972; Vergote et al., 1969).

4. Kohlberg (1981) says that our early stages of cognitive moral development are stages of punishment and obedience, focused on sanctions, rule keeping, and rule breaking. Is a God of judgment and sanctions rooted in these early ways of making moral sense of our human interactions.

5. Another suggestion, pieced together from many years of clinical work: suppose an infant or child is in intense psychic or physical pain and is left alone to make sense of that pain as best she can without much comfort from others (and the lack of comforting may be the worst part of the pain). She can make sense of the experience by either holding herself responsible or by blaming the external environment. Since the child is totally dependent on the external environment, blaming it and

thereby possibly being rejected by it may be too threatening for her. In that case, it makes more sense to blame herself, to say, I am in pain because I am bad or because there is something wrong with me. Thus begins the core of a sense of self-condemnation that like a snowball, will gather associations and grow larger throughout life. Thus the world is divided into two categories, one of which is me. I am bad and they are good, and because they are good, they must condemn me—a not unfamiliar stance to most clinicians and a stance that is echoed in many theologies.

Every child is vulnerable in a world that is larger and more complex than she can hope to master. Therefore every child encounters some failure and shame, and a judgmental God will resonate with her experience. If the family provides a safe and soothing environment, these fearful moments can be mastered and overcome. This "basic trust" (in Erikson's [1968] terminology) may be reflected in a child's sense of being held in the arms of God or watched over by a protective providence (for examples of this, see Rizzuto 1979). If the child's early milieu is not safe (emotionally and/or physically), as was the case for the three patients mentioned above, the terrors of childhood cannot be mastered and she grows up anxious or guilty. For this reason, as well as the others just mentioned, some children may naturally be drawn to a critical or judgmental God. Many encounter such a vision of God, but it does not take root in all of them. Many cast it off naturally as they grow up. It becomes deeply rooted only in those whose inner object world is congruent with such a God image.

6. Fairbairn (1943) describes the same phenomenon in what he calls the "moral defense" against bad object relations. As we have seen, Fairbairn believes the child internalizes painful and punishing objects in the hope of controlling them. One way in which this works, Fairbairn suggests, is to take the "badness"—the pain and grief associated with those objects—into oneself. This makes it possible for the child to regard the external objects as "good," since the child, not the parents or other external objects, is now felt to be the source of the pain and misery. Thus he sacrifices himself in order to save the system or, at least, to regard it as benign.

This is important since the child is totally dependent on his object world. If he experiences that world as arbitrary or destructive, a feeling of safety and security is impossible for him. The child must do everything he can to make that world seem safe, even if it means blaming himself for all the pain being experienced so that the outside world can remain guiltless and good.

Although he understands the dynamics differently than I do, Fairbairn is describing the same phenomenon when he writes, "the child would rather be bad himself than have bad objects. . . . one of his motives in becoming bad is to make his objects good. . . . he is rewarded by the sense of security which an environment of good objects so characteristically confers" (1943:66). And he concludes, "it is better to be a sinner in a world ruled by God than to live in a world ruled by the Devil" (1943:67).

In three of the cases reviewed above, then, the bond to a critical God served important dynamic functions: re-creating for Harold the experience of never being good enough; maintaining Sylvia in a state of depression and fragmentation; and providing Barbara with a relationship in which she could continually act out her feelings of guilt and shame. The attraction of this vision of God for these people, and for many others, was not accidental.

Later, through therapy or other encounters with more gracious relationships, the abused self may grow beyond paralyzing fear or guilt. As we saw above, this transformation of the self has an inevitable impact on the individual's bond with the sacred. A chronically angry God has no psychological function to perform for the more autonomous or cohesive self. Thus, as development resumes and the nature of the self's selfobject relationships change, this change is likely to be reflected in the person's relationship to his God. More specifically, a move from a fragmented and diminished sense of self toward a more autonomous and cohesive self might be mirrored in a shift from a vengeful to a nurturing deity— exactly what was observed in the three life histories presented above.

These reflections on judgmental and gracious representations of God suggest that people need an awareness that the ultimate nature of reality supports and legitimates their fundamental sense of themselves and undergirds their basic stance toward the world, even if it is cruel or uncaring.

The question remains whether or not such a punitive image of God is particularly suited to the dynamics of childhood. Does its presence in an adult represent the remains of a relic from childhood? Or is it possible for a person to have a reasonably strong and cohesive sense of self and still feel bound to a punishing and judging God? Such questions must be left to future investigations.

## *Summary: Self-Images and God Relationships*

In the transference, the patient's basic patterns of relating and making sense of experience are acted out and modified. It is hoped that this change will reverberate outside the consulting room to affect the patient's relations with friends, lovers, children, coworkers, and the sacred. In addition, the cases in this chapter have illustrated ways in which a major shift in an image of God or ultimate reality parallels the major breakthrough in the therapeutic relationship. Harold's passive stance was acted out both in relation to God and in the transference. When this shifted in the transference, it also shifted in relation to God. Sylvia's distant, impatient God, who she had to tell herself cared, paralleling her relationship with her parents, became a more accepting and caring God as she realized, in the transference, that someone could be patient with her. Barbara's experience of a judgmental, conditionally caring, guilt-inducing God shifted to a more accepting God as her defenses against caring were removed in the transference. Martin's experience of reality as cold and withholding and of truth as frustratingly unobtainable became more muted in the course of therapy as he became more open and accessible and began to experience the therapist as being available to him.

The previous chapter suggested that a relationship to a God might serve to ground our sense of who we are: the child who feels secure grounds that security in a caring God; the child who feels guilty and terrible grounds that sense of self by reference to a wrathful God. The child who feels estranged and isolated grounds that by reference to a cold and uncaring cosmos. These cases illustrate this possibility.

Before and after therapy, God remained the ultimate transferential ground of each person's sense of self. Harold was no longer the compliant "good boy" continually maintaining his sense of self by seeking the favor of others. Thus his God could no longer be the critical dictator who demanded thoughtless compliance. Sylvia was no longer the black sheep whom no one wanted. Thus her God could no longer be the aloof figure of her childhood. Barbara was no longer the guilty wretch, and so her God could no longer be primarily a figure of wrath and condemnation. The coming of a new sense of self in each case demanded a new image of God to ground it.

# CHAPTER

# 4

## TRANSFERENCE
## AND
## TRANSFORMATION

How is it possible for someone who has suffered extensive early damage to form a positive image of God? This question parallels the psychotherapeutic issue of the possibility for such people of forming a working alliance with the therapist and reworking their sense of self. The previous chapter described four patients and the parallels between changes occurring in the transference and transformations in their relationship to the sacred. This chapter will investigate whether the same dynamics function in both processes and how any parallels might illuminate the transformations that take place in and through religious practices.

The theories of change developed by James Masterson and Heinz Kohut will be critically evaluated and used as resources as I explore this topic, and I shall note the similarities and differences between their approaches. Transference is the major category in which psychotherapeutic change is understood psychoanalytically, and their theories of transference (and those of other contemporary analytic theorists) will form the framework for this discussion of psychotherapeutic and religious change.

## James Masterson

Masterson begins with what he calls the "real self," which he sees as the relatively healthy core of even the most disturbed personalities; it is the psychological center of the personality. As Masterson says, the "real self is used here not as the total self but in the intrapsychic sense of the sum of self and object representations with their related affects" (1985:21). In other words, it is the interior psychological source of our personality and behavior. The primary thrust of the real self is toward self-assertion and creativity. Its marks Masterson lists as spontaneity and aliveness of affect, self-entitlement, self-activation, assertion and support, acknowledgment of self-activation and maintenance of self-esteem, soothing of painful affects, continuity of self, commitment, and creativity (1985:26–27). Thus it is a real self in two senses: it represents the person's true identity, and it can deal directly with reality with a minimum of defensiveness.

Masterson calls his a developmental object relations perspective, which lays heavy emphasis on the separation-individuation model of development associated with Margaret Mahler (see Blanck and Blanck 1979). Writes Masterson, "my own theoretical perspective . . . placed major emphasis on the link between the gradual unfolding of the separation-individuation process and the growth and maturation of the self and object relations" (1985:17). Thus the natural human tendency is toward the development of real selfhood.

But this is not a totally intrapsychic process: it must be facilitated by the external environment. "This mirroring or matching process seems vital to the development of the real self . . . the capacity of the parents to perceive the unique characteristics of the child's emerging self and to respond to these in a positive, supportive manner" (1985:29). It is the parents' or caretaker's capacity to appreciate and encourage the uniqueness of the child that ensures that the real self will flourish rather than atrophy. Masterson quotes with approval the following statement by Mahler,

> I will assume the infant has two basic points of reference from which he builds up his self schema: one, his own inner feelings or states forming the

primitive core of the self on the one hand and, two, his sense of the care given by the libidinal object on the other hand. Insofar as the infant's development of the sense of self takes place in the context of the dependency on the mother, the sense of self that results will bear the imprint of her caregiving. (Mahler and McDevitt 1982:837; quoted in Masterson 1985:24)

Like Roland, Kohut, and others, Mahler and Masterson are here implying that it is the affective tone of the child's experiences—"his own inner feelings or states"—that form the core of the sense of self. It is these core affective states that are replayed in the transference and in all other relationships including the bond with the sacred. Masterson comments on this passage in words that could have been written by Kohut: "I understand this to mean the mother's capacity to acknowledge and respond with support to the unique emerging self. . . . the caregiver's mirroring is a most important ingredient in the development of the sense of self" (1985:24).

If such empathic mirroring does not take place, if the child in her development is neglected, rejected, or emotionally traumatized, she experiences what Masterson calls "abandonment depression," a mixture of "depression, guilt, helplessness and hopelessness, and massive rage which was also heavily defended against, and an absence of any feeling of self-entitlement" (1985:40). Even if the child is provided with food, shelter, and some human contact, she can still feel "abandoned" if she is seen only as an extension of the parents or is treated with coldness and disdain.

To defend against that pain, the child builds a defensive self. Masterson's distinction between the real self and the defensive self has some resonance to Winnicott's ([1960] 1965) distinction of true and false selves, but for Winnicott the "false self" may be quite adaptive and protective and not a defense against pain or depression. (Further discussion of this Winnicottian concept can be found in Bollas [1989] and Phillips [1988].)

According to Masterson, the defensive self can take basically two forms: seeing oneself as a helpless child who will be rewarded only for conformity with everyone else's wishes or seeing oneself as a bad child who is to blame for the emotional (and physical) abuse one is receiving.

In Masterson's words, "defensive self-representations . . . consist of two equally unrealistic fantasy images: that of a helpless child who is loved and rewarded for not asserting himself and an inadequate, evil bad self which impels the mother to withdraw" (1985:32). In either case, the child fears that genuine self-expression will be punished with abandonment, and these two stances are designed to ward off that possibility or the memory of its past occurrences. Just as the parents emotionally, if not physically, abandoned the child, so the child learns to abandon his real self until the question becomes, as Masterson puts it, "does the patient feel confident enough about the real self to identify what he or she wants and experiment with reality to fulfill it?" (1985:15).

A person who has identified himself with these defensive self-images is virtually incapable of trust and intimacy. Any close relationship touches the abandonment depression and so engages the feelings of being either a helpless obedient child or a bad person or both. He also believes that genuine self-disclosure will again precipitate abandonment and so fears that if someone really knows him, rejection is sure to follow.

Masterson calls this "the borderline triad—activation of the real self or individuation leads to depression which leads to defense"—that is, to engagement of the defensive selves (1985:41, 80). Being oneself within a relationship is associated with abandonment and "with extremely painful affects of depression, rage, hopelessness and helplessness" (1985:85). So any move toward intimacy, individuation, or self-assertion provokes these feelings of abandonment, which then engage the false selves as defenses against this painful affect. The person then becomes passive and compliant or depressed and self-critical or both.

Inevitably the process of connecting and reconnecting is hindered. The defensive self is terrified to connect with others (and perhaps with God as well) except on the basis of being either a helpless and dependent child or an evil creature constantly on the verge of rejection. We might note in passing how much religious language pulls for either or both of these defensive postures: the believer is to be a helpless and dependent child and/or an evil creature constantly under the threat of divine punishment, a point I will return to later.

Beneath all these defenses, the real self that can engage in genuine relationships without defensiveness remains hidden. Implicit in Masterson's theories, although it is rarely made explicit, is an understanding of intimacy and relationships very similar to that implied in the work of Erik Erikson. Erikson's (1968) developmental schema implies that identity (the task of adolescence) must come before intimacy (the task of early adulthood). Similarly, for Masterson, authentic connections with persons (and other objects) must be grounded in the real self, and he explicitly connects his understanding of real selfhood to Erikson's notion of self-identity (1985:28). Only if intimacy grows from the real self can it be nondefensive and based on a realistic view of the other.

Masterson's therapy consists of several stages. First, the defensive self and its maneuvers must be confronted. For example, in one case study Masterson writes that the "treatment plan was to confront the maladaptive or self-destructive aspects of her avoidance of real-self activation and the operations of her defensive self" (1985:41). This direct confrontation with the patient's defensive self is the core of Masterson's approach to therapy, for "the patient, relying on his defensive self, avoids real-self activation, denying the price he pays in reality for this avoidance. The therapist confronts the borderline patient's defensive self . . . as a defense against the abandonment depression" (1985:59).

But it must be remembered that these defenses have served to hold back waves of pain. Once the defenses begin to come down, those almost overpowering affects flood the patient's psyche. "The therapist's confrontation brings both the abandonment depression and the difficulties of the real self's functioning to the center stage of treatment" (1985:42). Thus, therapy must provide a safe place where the nearly overwhelming emotions tied up in the abandonment depression can be experienced and grieved through. Masterson suggests that once the rage and grief begin to subside, the real self that "lies dormant or latent behind or beneath the defensive self" begins to emerge. One sign of this is that the patient takes up some activity that represents genuine self-expression. At this point, Masterson recommends the therapist go beyond the traditional analytic stance of neutrality and support the emergence of the real self in a process he calls "communicative matching."

> Efforts to overcome the difficulty with real-self expression go hand in hand
> with working through the depression. Each patient usually selects on his

own an activity as a vehicle to facilitate this development. . . . The patient's efforts at self-activation meet success, which is followed by depression at the temporary surrender of the defensive self, followed by the reactivation of the defensive self. . . . It is at this point the therapist should introduce his communicative matching interventions. (1985:60).

This more active stance on the therapist's part is necessary because "the real self will not emerge and fully assume its capacities without acknowledgment from the environment. Failure to be acknowledged had a great deal to do with its impairment in early development and the therapist's intervention in treatment helps to overcome the impairment" (1985:63).

Thus therapy reverses the developmental trajectory and the patient works back behind the defensive selves and through the despair of abandonment to the real self. The therapeutic relationship then supplies a safe place in which genuine self development can begin again. Treatment should lead "to overcoming the defenses and working through the abandonment depression, which attenuated or overcame the developmental arrest so that the separation individuation process could resume its developmental path" (1985:17).

Like Kohut's, Masterson's therapy is a psychology of developmental arrests, but the understanding of development is fundamentally different. For Masterson, development, in and out of therapy, is a process of separation-individuation. Like most object relations theorists, Masterson emphasizes autonomy as the goal of development.

Although Masterson approvingly quotes Erikson's notion of identity as similar to his image of the real self, conspicuously absent from his list of the capabilities of the real self (1985:26) are Erikson's concern for intimacy, caring, and giving the self away. Both Masterson and Mahler, whom he relies on extensively, seem so preoccupied with the self's struggle for independence and the threat posed by the encroachments of (primarily) the mother that they focus almost exclusively on the acquisition of a virtually isolated and self-sustaining individuality. They tend to overlook the turning of the self toward an other and others in self-giving, perhaps out of fear that such a turn represents a return to the smothering enmeshments of childhood. How common in psychoanalytic theory is this single-minded focus on autonomy and the fear (which was Freud's as well) that relationships must mean the loss of individuality. Thus the deep structure of going out and returning that undergirds Erikson's work is short-circuited or relegated to childhood before the development of autonomy.

This, then, becomes for Masterson his main difference from Kohut, whose theory, Masterson writes, "competes with object relations theory and seems to run contrary to the findings of child observation research that the self separates from the object. . . . [This] leads to conceptual confusions between the self and the object as part of the self" (1985:16). Whether Kohut's framework is "contrary to the findings of child observation" is an issue discussed by Stern (1985), who reviews the research on infant development and finds that it does not support the Mahler-Masterson sequence of developmental stages. Stern's findings are, in fact, more compatible with Kohut's schema, a fact Stern himself notes (1985:242). I will turn to Stern's research shortly.

It is true that Kohut's terminology of "selfobject," "self-selfobject," and so on is confusing in this regard. But Masterson's objection seems based on a significant misunderstanding of Kohut when he continually refers to Kohut's theory as one of "fused self objects." Kohut is clearly not speaking of fusion in a Mahlerian sense but rather of a relationship that contains real bonding while also preserving individuality. Such a relationship is incomprehensible in the categories of Mahler's theory of separation-individuation which dichotomizes the possibilities as either fusion or autonomy. What Masterson seems to object to is that for Kohut the self is always interdependent and never becomes completely autonomous, whereas Masterson insists upon autonomy as the mark of mental health and the overriding goal of treatment.

## Heinz Kohut

It would seem that for Kohut there must be some internal drive toward the development of the self, since "the self and the survival of its nuclear program is the basic force in everyone's personality" (1984:147). As we have discussed earlier, this dynamic is facilitated or thwarted according to the selfobject milieu of the subject. "Even hatred is . . . sustaining. What leads to the human self's destruction, however, is its exposure to the coldness, the indifference of the nonhuman, nonempathically responding world" (1984:18).

For Kohut there is a reverse parallel between the origin and the cure of psychopathology. Just as "all forms of psychopathology . . . are due to disturbances of selfobject relationships in childhood" (1984:53), so the cure of all forms of psychopathology can be located in the provision of more positive selfobject relationships in the present. More specifically, the structure of the self depends on the nature of the selfobject bond, and if that relationship is disturbed, the person "does not acquire the needed internal structure, [and] his psyche remains fixated on an archaic selfobject" (1971:45). For such traumatized souls, all contemporary relationships are evaluated in terms of the availability of narcissistic supplies. Although all of us depend on selfobject relationships to sustain our identities, the severely traumatized exhibit "what seems to be an intense form of object hunger. The intensity of the search for and dependency on these objects is due to the fact that they are striven for as a substitute for the missing segments of the psychic structure" (1971:45). Their dependency is much more global and emotionally driven and their sense of self much more fragile.

How often, we might ask in passing, is a bond with the sacred used to fill these unmet archaic selfobject dependencies? For example, Kohut writes, "persons who have suffered such traumas are . . . forever attempting to achieve a union with an idealized object since, in view of their structural defect . . . their narcissistic equilibrium is safeguarded only through the interest, the responses, and the approval of present-day replicas of the traumatically lost selfobject" (1971:55). An idealized but punitive God representation precisely fits that need—exactly the dynamic we saw operative in the cases of Barbara and Sylvia to whom we will return shortly. Kohut also notes that such people, lacking self-structure, are dependent on external selfobjects not only for sustenance but for their very sense of self. "Since all bliss and power now reside in the idealized object, the child feels empty and powerless when he is separated from it" (1971:37). Thus these people are easily drawn into religious groups that demand absolute loyalty and dependency.

Therapy is possible because empathic and in-tuned selfobject bonds remobilize that stalled developmental process. Kohut writes that his is a "theory of thwarted and remobilized self development responding to self development–thwarting and self development-enhancing selfobjects" (1984:142). This restarted developmental process makes it possible for therapy to create a new psychic structure through empathic atunement and optimal frustration. "We define therapeutic progress toward mental health not primarily by reference to expanded knowledge or increased ego autonomy, but by reference to the laying down of permanent self structures via optimal frustration" (1984:153). This more cohesive self, however, is thereby rendered not more autonomous and independent but more able to use mature rather than infantile selfobject relations; that is, the self is now "increasingly able to evoke the empathic resonance of mature selfobjects and to be sustained by them" (1984:66). For, Kohut writes,

> throughout his life a person will experience himself as a cohesive harmonious firm unit in time and space, connecting with its past and pointing meaningfully into a creative-productive future [but] only as long as, at each stage in his life, he experiences certain representatives of his human surroundings as joyfully responding to him, as available to him as sources of idealized strength and calmness, as being silently present but in essence like him, and, at any rate, able to grasp his inner life more or less accurately so that their responses are attuned to his needs. (1984:52)

Therapy does not make us less dependent of others but rather makes healthy dependency more likely.

Presumably this newfound capacity might be reflected in a new relationship to the cosmic or the sacred as well as to friends, lovers, colleagues, and clients. For the three basic selfobject needs—"the need to be confirmed in its vitality and assertiveness by the mirroring selfobject, to be calmed and uplifted by the idealized imago, or to be surrounded by the quietly sustaining presence of alter egos" (1984:23)—might well be met in part through a cosmic connection, and religions have often served as sources of mirroring and valuing. And personal transformations in the religious domain might be understood in terms of the shifting selfobject function of the sacred.

Therapy, then, reverses the traumatic trajectory and provides a place where the self-structuring process can begin again, by "the opening of a path of empathy between self and selfobject, specifically the establishment of empathic in-tuneness between self and selfobject. This new channel of empathy permanently takes the place of the formerly repressed or split off archaic narcissistic relationship; it supplants the bondage that had formerly tied the archaic self to the archaic selfobject" (1984:66). Bondage to more primitive forms of selfobject relations is a function of unmet selfobject needs. When those needs are met in the selfobject transference with the therapist or with other selfobjects, the self is free to outgrow these more self-destructive and enslaving forms of interaction. Or, in Kohut's words, "the analysand's formerly archaic needs for the responses of archaic selfobjects are superseded by the experience of the availability of empathic resonance" (1984:77).

Since this healing process takes place only in the context of a relationship, the contrast is not between freedom and dependency but only between immature (archaically bonded) and mature forms of dependency, mature dependency being that which, paradoxically, nurtures freedom and autonomy.

Thus Masterson is correct. The differences between his approach and Kohut's rest upon fundamentally different models of the course and goal of human development. Masterson envisions a linear movement culminating in a state of "separation-individuation." Kohut insists that "a move from dependency (symbiosis) to independence (autonomy) is an impossibility and that the developmental moves of normal psychological life must be seen in the changing nature of the relationships between the self and its selfobjects" (1984:52). And these different models of development reflect radically different conceptions of human nature: the eternally autonomous individual or the continually interconnected self.

Masterson's model of cure involves a heroic breaking through of the defensive barriers and the setting free of the imprisoned real self. It is a work of confrontation and rescue in which a captive is given freedom and autonomy. Kohut's cure involves creating an interpersonal matrix in which a new self is nurtured into being through a carefully balanced blend of love and discipline. It is a work of reparenting.

## *Daniel Stern*

Masterson framed his difference from Kohut in terms of the study of infant development. A practicing psychoanalyst and specialist in infant research, Daniel Stern, reviewed findings in infant development with an eye to their clinical implications in his book *The Interpersonal World of the Infant* (1985). Through extremely close observation of infants' actions, responses, recognitions, and other behavior, Stern concluded that a rudimentary sense of self is present from the beginning. (In organizing his book around the development of a sense of self rather than the acquisition of autonomy, Stern is implicitly agreeing with Kohut that the central clinical issue, at least today, is not autonomy but cohesive selfhood.) According to Stern, what is laid down in early childhood is not a series of developmental stages progressing from symbiosis to autonomy but rather sets of interpersonal interactions. For Stern, the infant is interpersonal rather than fused from birth with an elementary capacity to initiate action, evoke responses in others, and respond to their responses. Entry into the world is entry into a mutually reciprocal interpersonal field, and later development only enriches and complexifies what is there from the beginning.

The infant is dependent on caretakers who regulate her functions: when to eat, sleep, interact, and so on. And Stern reiterates a point crucial to my earlier discussion of transference, that it is "clear that strong feelings and important representations are forged not necessarily by the very acts of being fed or put to sleep . . . but rather by the manner in which these acts are performed" (1985:104). For example, the institutionalized infants whom Spitz (1945, 1946) studied were adequately fed and clothed, but they failed to thrive because they failed to receive even a minimum of interpersonal contact. And in the nonhuman world, the Harlows' (1969) studies of baby monkeys indicated that a cloth mother surrogate was no substitute for a real mother regardless of how well fed the babies were.

Feeding, putting to bed, changing diapers, not only relieve physiological distress, then; the manner in which they are done lays down certain interpersonal patterns and expectations. Such simple acts of child care are not only biological but interpersonal. And the interpersonal lessons the child learns from them persist long after he has learned to feed and clothe himself. According to Stern, these units of interaction generalize and become the building blocks of later interpersonal relations. Thus he calls them RIGs—"Representations of Interactions that have been Generalized." In what could stand as a summary of his approach, Stern writes:

> Our interest concerns not only the actions [of caretaking] but also the sensations and affects. What we are concerned with, then, are episodes that involve interpersonal interactions of different types. Further, we are concerned with the interactive experience, not just the interactive events. I am suggesting that these episodes are also averaged and represented preverbally. They are Representations of Interactions that have been Generalized (1985:97).

Our core sense of self is built out of these RIGs which are, according to Stern, combined into what he calls working models of "who I am, who my mother is, what I can expect from my environment," and so on. Although the term *working model* (which also occurs in attachment theory in a more restricted sense) sounds cognitive, Stern makes clear that our basic interpersonal experiences and the sense of self we derive from them involve not just the processing of cognitive information but also such things as the "arousal, affect, mastery, physiological state, state of consciousness, and curiosity" (1985:115) that the infant experiences in the presence of another person.

Rather than viewing the formation of cognitive schemata as basic to the sense of self and others, Stern emphasizes the importance of shared affect (or lack of it) in the formation of interpersonal experience, coining the term *interaffectivity* and suggesting that "interaffectivity may be the first, most pervasive, and most immediately important form of sharing subjective experiences" (1985:132). And he devotes a central chapter to the necessity of what he calls "affective attunement" in the development of a strong sense of self (1985:138–161). Clearly his notion of "affective attunement" is very similar to Kohut's idea of empathy. Although Stern explicitly recognizes the similarities of his conclusions and Kohut's (reached by very different routes) regarding the centrality of empathy in the development of a sense of self, he neither affirms nor rejects the controversial Kohutian insistence on the centrality of empathy in psychotherapeutic treatment (1985:219–220).

For Stern, then, "the infant's life is so thoroughly social that most of the things the infant does, feels, and perceives occur in different kinds of relationships" (1985:118). Even speech is considered important not primarily in terms of the cognitive capacity to transmit information but "in terms of forming shared experiences, of reestablishing the 'personal order,' of creating a new type of 'being-with'" (1985:172). Rather than the atomistic autonomy envisioned as the goal of child development (and treatment) in Mahler's theory, Stern asserts that human life is fundamentally interpersonal from beginning to end. In terms of the theoretical dichotomy between Masterson and Kohut basic to this chapter, Stern suggests that "the more one conceives of intersubjective relatedness as a basic psychological need, the closer one refashions clinical theory toward the configurations suggested by self psychologists and some existential psychologists" (1985:136).

In addition, the research reviewed by Stern regarding the importance of the *affective bond* in human development strengthens the central contention of this book regarding the importance of the affective bond in understanding transference phenomena including psychotherapeutic treatment, interpersonal relations, and religious experience. Early Representations of Interactions may Generalize beyond parents and siblings and spouses and friends and offspring to touch even our relationship to the cosmos and to the divine.

The differences between Kohut and Masterson, Mahler and Stern, illustrate the way in which psychological theories are also moral systems, a theme recently receiving attention in both the psychological literature (Bergin 1980) and the field of religious studies (Browning [1988] includes a discussion of this aspect of Kohut and other contemporary psychologists). Models of health are inherently normative, prescribing some actions and proscribing others. Like all psychotherapeutic systems, Masterson's and Kohut's are necessarily teleological, proposing an ideal human type to strive for: the self-assertive and autonomous individual (Masterson 1985:26–29) or the self able to rely on and be sustained by interpersonal relationships (Kohut 1984:49–63).

These two models of human nature—the self-contained self and the interpersonal self—have significantly different implications for the study and practice of religion. The first is apt to view religion as a threat to human autonomy (Freud would be a primary example of this stance) or to construct a religion and morality in which the autonomous individual is the primary unit (the approach of the philosopher Immanuel Kant). Since some dependency is seen as necessary and inevitable in human life, the second model does not reject religion and morality out of hand (for example, see Kohut [1984:76] for his discussion of his difference from Freud on this point) and might provide the resources for a religious vision in which interconnection to a sacred reality becomes central (a suggestion I will return to in the last chapter).

The philosophical anthropologies implicit in the works of Mahler and Stern need not be seen as irreconcilable, although Stern himself continually underscores his differences with Mahler (for example, in 1985, pt. 3). But Stern's findings do qualify Mahler's schema by locating it in a larger context. It remains true that the infant develops from relative dependency to relative autonomy (but not from some kind of total fusion as conveyed by the term *symbiosis* to some kind of radical autonomy conjured up by the term *separation-individuation*). But more important, this movement from relative dependency to relative autonomy continues in the context of an interpersonal matrix. And the drive for relative autonomy is not antagonistic to interpersonal bonds; rather, as Kohut insists, strong selfobject connections are the necessary preconditions for developing the high degree of relative autonomy of which human beings are capable. Without them, the self remains fragmented and thus neurotically dependent. Autonomy, then, becomes a relational concept.

The moral vision that emerges from this model of human nature as relatively autonomous but continually embedded in interpersonal networks refuses to condemn all dependency and connection but rather suggests a differentiation between neurotic and healthy dependencies. Neurotic dependencies would be those that keep the self fragmented, whereas healthy dependencies would be those that support self-development and relative autonomy. The following discussion of the four cases, while focusing on the process of psychotherapeutic and religious transformation, will indirectly illustrate how these criteria might apply to various religious forms.

## *Transformations*

Masterson is much more straightforward than many other like-minded theoreticians in affirming the presence of a relatively normal and healthy real self at the center of even the most disturbed personality. Transformation involves breaking through the defensive selves and liberating the inner real self. Both forms of defensive selfhood—the totally compliant child and the evil person—find their resonances in many religions. They encourage their members to assume one or both of these self-destructive postures and readily provide an image of God to serve as the transferential ground of the devotee's identifications with these defensive personae.

For example, Harold, the passive banker, found the image of God as the cosmic scorekeeper congruent with his compliant defensive self. In relation to such a God he could reenact the same pattern that undergirded his doomed marriage: he could remain eternally the pleaser, vainly trying to satisfy one who would always find fault. Thus this script, which had begun in relation to his mother, would play forever in relation to a distant and critical deity. It was his destiny and the destiny of the human race as his church taught it to remain forever in a state of passive infantile obedience, struggling to surrender more and more areas of self-assertion in conformity to a virtually endless list of divine prohibitions. Thus his religion promised him the chance to remain eternally identified with a compliant defensive self free from ever taking the risk and responsibility of self-assertion. He was taught that such "selfishness" would bring the wrath of God upon him. And so it would. He knew from his own experience that initiative brought with it the fires of conscience stoked by the pain of the abandonment depression behind his defensive compliance. Martha, his ex-wife, he once told me, insisted

that the towels be folded and put away in exactly this one way. Not only did they have to be folded in precisely the correct size but they had to be stacked on the shelves in the right order by color. I once tried to tell her that I thought this was absurd, but she flew into a rage and delivered me a lecture on the importance of order. It was really important to her. Once it took me so long to fold the towels to exactly the proper size that I didn't have time to put them back in the right sequence before leaving for work.

All day long I was unable to concentrate. I felt guilty and agitated because I had done it wrong. It was a lost day on the job. I rushed home in a panic and fortunately got there before she did and so could rearrange them and get them back right. We've been separated a year and I have my own apartment and I still feel upset and guilty when I put my towels in the closet the way I want rather than the way Martha would have me do it.

The thought of noncompliance to even the most ridiculous of demands engaged the abandonment rage and plunged him into hell—the hell of those painful affects from the past masquerading as conscience. Neither his marriage nor his church questioned this extreme passivity or provided a place where the rage and grief behind it might be worked through. Rather, both were willing to play on it for their own purposes and to deepen his identification with this defensive self with scoldings about what the good husband or the true believer should be like.

The divorce forced him into therapy, and therapy forced him to confront the cost to himself of his extreme passivity. Harold was so identified with this compliant persona that he had no idea what he really liked or wanted in most situations, and cut off from his real self, he could not tap the energy to act to obtain it, even if he knew what it was he wanted.

So the first part of therapy was punctuated by my continually asking him, "Harold," what do *you* want to do with your sons?" or "How do *you* want to handle that work situation?" Gradually it dawned on him that he had no answers to those questions because no one had ever asked him before (except, perhaps, in a sarcastic tone of voice), and so he had never learned how to pay attention to his interests and desires.

That realization inflamed him and weeks of rage ensued. Again he was amazed that I respected and encouraged his angry feelings and continually pointed out how understandable they were, given the way that he had lived. To help him work this out, as well as to improve his self-confidence, Harold took up racketball as an outlet.

As the rage subsided, he expressed interest in finding a new job, and we worked together as he located a "headhunter" and prepared for a series of interviews that culminated in a new position. Along the way he rediscovered an interest in music and took up piano playing again. (Martha had always criticized his interest in the piano as "sissy stuff.")

The Harold that left therapy was a far cry from the Harold who first appeared in my office. By dropping his compliant façade and mobilizing his real self, he was able to change jobs, hire a new lawyer, renegotiate his divorce settlement, and win joint custody of his two boys. These transformations and reworkings of his sense of self were comprehensible in terms of Masterson's model of change. And a theory that stresses autonomy as the goal of treatment was appropriate for someone who had been so dependent throughout his life.

In the process of therapy, Harold reworked his relationship to his God, even though that was never a direct object of intervention. The shattering of the defensive self meant that an eternally demanding God was no longer necessary. Nor was there any longer a need to re-create a transference bond in which Harold continually played the compliant child. The dissipation of the abandonment rage cooled the fires of conscience that had continually seared his every attempt to take the initiative.

The God that emerged at the end was a God much more in keeping with Harold's newly released real selfhood. Still a God of morality, this new God wrote his covenant on the heart. Harold was responsible for finding it and expressing it out of a sense of autonomous responsibility rather than servile fear. Harold's new God delighted in Harold's maximizing his talents rather than burying them beneath layers of passivity and compliance.

The change that took place in Harold's religion was not that he simply adopted a new religious ideology, although it might look that way on the surface. Many in his church, as they heard him talk about his faith and his ideas of God, considered him an apostate as he spoke out against their wrathful deity. Masterson writes about the negative reaction of peers to a person's real self becoming actualized: "The borderline disordered self would react to the positive forces [those movements in society and changes in others that 'reinforce and potentiate self expression'] not with greater real self expression but with greater anxiety about real self expression. It would react to the negative forces [those movements that impair self-expression] as a reinforcement of its pathological defenses" (1985:105). Over the years I have occasionally treated patients who have left cults and seen the harassment they have received from their former compatriots. This is an extreme form of the reaction against someone who attempts further individuation by those who remain compliant. In Harold's case the complaints against him were raised at the doctrinal level, but these disputes clearly carried other, psychological issues.

But to Harold such a God no longer made sense of his experience of himself and his relations in the world. As Harold told me toward the end of therapy:

> I know how destructive it is to live under that kind of punishing regime. I am a parent and I would never, ever treat my children that way. I've learned my lesson and what it's done to me. I could never do that to them. If I know better than that, surely God does. God is surely even a better parent than I am.

Harold's sense of a God that required responsibility rather than slavery was more than just a creedal change; it grew from a profound transformation in his sense of himself. He told me:

> The real heart of morality is taking responsibility. That's what I want my kids to learn. That's what I've learned in this class I'm teaching in the church on business ethics. In business I'm facing situations that don't fit neatly into any rule book. All I have to go on is my sense of personal responsibility. It's really true that only my conscience can be my guide. And I could never develop that sense of responsibility if I'm never given any responsibility. If my whole life is just planned out for me every step of the way, I'll never learn to take responsibility or make decisions. If all I have to do is follow the program, I'm just a piece of machinery, I'm just like the computer on my desk; that's not being a son of God.

This religious transformation from devotion to a demanding God to belief in a God of personal responsibility reflects a deep psychological shift from identification with a defensive self to the actualization of the real self. In this transition the central themes of Harold's faith—God as parent, God as source of morality—remain but they are significantly redefined. His God is no longer a demanding and controlling parent but rather one who respects and encourages initiative. Morality no longer means blindly following rules but rather developing a personal conscience and sense of responsibility. In keeping with the actualization of real selfhood, at the close of treatment Harold's was a God who could ground his moral autonomy.

For Kohut, treatment works not by liberating the real self but by creating new self-structures through the internalization of empathic experiences with the therapist. Rather than individual autonomy, the goal is more sustaining and enhancing relationships.

For example, Sylvia and Barbara, both of whom had been abused as children, found in the wrathful deities of their adolescence Gods who would support their sense that there was something terribly and incurably wrong with themselves. The preaching and teaching of their churches focused on the core issue of their lives—guilt and forgiveness. But this issue was addressed in a way that produced feelings of condemnation rather than forgiveness.

I once had a similar experience myself. Driving late at night with the radio as my companion on a trip across the state of Indiana, the only station I could find was local religious broadcasting. A preacher was holding forth, and so I became, for an hour or so, his captive parishioner. He was preaching on forgiveness. But the more I listened, the guiltier I felt. Strange, I thought, he's talking about forgiveness but he's making me feel guilty. Cynically, I began to wonder if his religion was not producing the very disease of guilt that he was claiming to cure.

This theological sleight of hand involved using the language of forgiveness but placing all the emphasis on a God of wrathful condemnation. Such an image of God encourages the kind of relationship in which a devotee can reenact the experience of being judged and found guilty. Often people who are abused feel guilty, partly because they imagine they played some role in the abuse and partly because they turn the blame and anger on themselves.

In Masterson's terms, one way of warding off the pain and rage from such abuse is to experience oneself as horrible and to identify oneself as evil and therefore deserving of abuse. Sylvia's childhood faith provided a ready language in which to express this defensive self. Her pastor continually described the human race as a gathering of "rotten worms," Sylvia told me once, loosely translating from her native language. She was often praised for the long periods of fasting she undertook as a child in a hopeless attempt to purify herself of the guilt she felt. But at the end of each fast, she would feel only that she hadn't done enough.

As mentioned before Fairbairn refers to this dynamic as the "moral defense against bad objects"—"the child would rather be bad himself than have bad objects." And so the child "takes upon himself the burden of badness that appears to reside in his objects,"—and in becoming bad himself, makes the others in his world good (1943:65). It feels safer to live in a world governed by good forces, even if the subject must feel bad about herself, than to live in a world apparently governed by evil forces. As Fairbairn puts it, "it is better to be a sinner in a world ruled by God than to live in a world ruled by the Devil" (1943:66). Sylvia's family religion was skilled at playing on this dynamic. In many ways she was told that the price of living in a world ruled by God was to totally abase herself.

And, of course, such abusive interactions do not allow basic selfobject needs to be met or self-cohesion to develop. Thus the self remains prone to depression and feelings of fragmentation (Kohut 1971). Depression was the presenting complaint for Sylvia (and for Barbara). Her religious fellowships failed to provide the warm and empathic selfobject milieu that would allow her development. All the theoreticians discussed in this book concur that it is the emotional tenor of the early interactions rather than their cognitive content that shapes or distorts self-development. Although the language of Sylvia's faith was the language of love and forgiveness, it was spoken in a context tinctured by anger and rejection, and those were the experiences she internalized.

So Sylvia entered early adolescence as a shy girl with a guilty secret that she was afraid to tell even to God, so convinced was she of his wrath. Her only hope lay in "holiness," trying to make herself pure ("with the help of God, of course," she threw in as an afterthought). But that, of course, was impossible for a sinner like herself, forever soiled by her incestuous past. It was her destiny, and the destiny of the human race as her church taught it, to try and fail and forever feel not good enough. Even the doctrine of the forgiveness of sins that might, in the hands of a more gracious God, have put an end to this Sisyphean cycle of condemnation was interpreted in her tradition to mean simply that she might start over and over again, but she could never trust that she would be so forgiven that she would be at peace.

In my experience, Sylvia was not alone in this. Over the years I worked with many patients from highly religious backgrounds, and the more they talked about how their sins had been washed away, the more burdened by sin they seemed to feel. The more they swam in the river of forgiveness, the more they seemed to be drowning in guilt.

The central thrust of Sylvia's treatment was my communicating to her that I could understand and accept her—with her past. But although she desperately wanted my acceptance, she resisted it in many ways. "You don't mean it," she would say. "It's just your job." Or, "You don't really know me. If you did, then you would hate me too."

It took many, many months of this psychic arm-wrestling before Sylvia began to experience being understood. Only in that context could she begin the process of facing what had happened to her and working through the feelings associated with it. Simply talking about "love" and "acceptance" meant nothing to her. Years spent in a family and church that had freely used the words but in a milieu of coldness and criticism had inoculated her against them. Rather it was the experience of another person struggling to see things through her eyes that opened up for her the possibility that her isolation could be penetrated and she could be seen and not judged. This was an experience that later could be incorporated into her developing sense of self.

According to Kohut, then, change takes place because new and more gracious interpersonal experiences are internalized as new psychological structures. And these new structures make new and more fruitful relationships possible. These changes, in turn, reverberate through a person's relationship to the sacred.

Rejected by her family and condemned by her God for events over which she had no control, Sylvia entered therapy anxious and depressed. She needed less a God who would ground her strivings for autonomy and more a God who would serve as an empathic and resonant selfobject. But she lacked the self-structure needed to connect with mirroring and gracious selfobjects, either human or divine. Kohut once wrote, "We must have a healthy biological apparatus in order to utilize the oxygen that surrounds us. . . . Similarly, we must be in possession of available nuclear self-esteem . . . in order to seek out mirroring selfobjects and be nourished by their response to us" (1984:77).

As therapy progressed, Sylvia was more able to accept and incorporate the understanding shown by the therapist and the affection shown by her friends, and this eventually made a new relationship to God possible. This dynamic explains why, when I asked her if God's love helped her accept herself, she said, "No, it was the other way around. Only after I accepted myself could I accept that God and others cared."

An aloof, angry God made it possible for Sylvia to keep her needs for mirroring and empathy split off, along with (following Masterson) the pain and anger associated with their betrayal. And keeping those needs and feelings repressed enabled her to remain the dutiful self-sacrificing child her family and faith demanded. Her unmerciful demanding God continued to represent the lack of those selfobject resources necessary to develop a strong and integrated self and grow beyond her archaic needs.

Once those needs were met in therapy, the development of the self began again. Incorporating the therapist's concern made a more gracious relationship to herself possible, enabling her to draw on the support of her friends and to recognize her abilities and achievements. Thus she no longer needed (or wanted) the archaic tie to punishing and fragmenting selfobjects. Sylvia separated decisively from her family by ceasing to apologize for leaving home and refusing to tolerate their verbal abuse, from her earlier religion by joining another church, and from her childhood deity by opening herself to a new vision of God. She told me at the close of therapy:

> I see God as more forgiving. I see parts of Scripture about God's love that I never saw before. One of my favorite Bible stories used to be God's punishment on Sodom and Gomorrah. I remember having that, and the story of the Flood, read to me over and over again as a child. But the other day I noticed that God repented of destroying the world and that he says in Isaiah that he has written my name on the palm of his hand. I cried when I read those words. If God can face and repent of his destructiveness, why can't my pastor and my family? Why didn't anyone tell me that God has engraved my name on his hand where he'll never forget me?

A cohesive and productive self is one pole of a set of empathic and nurturing selfobject relations. Developing an integrated self required more congenial selfobject bonds. So Sylvia withdrew from a family who abused her, friends who took advantage of her, and a God who battered her. An empathic and sustaining deity was more appropriate to her stronger sense of self.

Therapeutically, how did Martin's changes come about? Did Martin uncover a buried real self or generate new self structures out of the therapeutic relationship?

Here too the transference played a crucial role in the treatment but in a way rather different from that envisioned by Kohut and Masterson. Working through his anger in the transference started the change that took place. At first, I responded to Martin's sarcastic remarks about others by commenting on his anger, but he would deny that he was angry and say that he was just objectively evaluating their work. So I dropped that tactic until a more trusting relationship could develop. Only after sometime in therapy could he start to direct some of his anger at me by making sarcastic remarks first about psychology in general—"A bastard discipline, neither a humanities nor a science"—and then about my office—"How can you find anything in that awful mess that passes for your desk?"—and then about my style—"I'll bet you forgot what we talked about last time." Fortunately I was able to respond without becoming too defensive: I half agreed with him about psychology, I certainly agreed with him about the condition of my desktop, and I could appreciate his concern about my powers of memory and concentration.

Rather than defending myself or attacking him—the two responses he was most familiar with—I encouraged him to express his anger and frustration at having to consult a psychologist and one with a messy desk who sometimes seemed distracted. Only after the bond between us was stronger could Martin begin to acknowledge his anger. As he did so, he also began to realize how he kept me at a distance by keeping his feelings to himself, something, to be sure, he had not done consciously.

But working through his anger was not an end in itself; treatment was not just an emotional release or a grieving process. The very experience of the transference, of being in a relationship that could contain his anger, had a profound impact upon Martin. In the more responsive therapeutic relationship, he could relax the struggle, let down his guard, and use his remarkable powers of perception to see what his own life had been about rather than constantly diverting himself by intellectual battles.

> I just can't believe it. It's hard to accept the way my early life has repeated itself in my work. Yet it's the same thing—trying to find the impossible dream, the perfect parent or the absolute truth. It's even harder to accept that I can't have it. My parents are so involved in their careers, they'll never be parents. They'll go to their grave never knowing who I am or what effect they had on me. They're proud, of course, because I'm such an intellectual. They take credit for that. As if being an intellectual was just a matter of training. They'll never know the deeper impact of their lives on my life. For a while I thought I couldn't live without it. Without parents. Without an absolute, final truth about the human condition, about the meaning of literature, the destiny of the creative spirit. Without an absolutely true interpretation of the meaning of the novel—not just a particular novel but THE NOVEL in capital letters—an absolutely true understanding with which I could bludgeon my opponents into submission. But I can't have it. There's no such thing. There's just process—to use your word, I can't believe I'm talking such psychobabble—but it's true, there's just process, interaction, discussion. A Socratic dialogue, a Platonic symposium, a Hegelian dialectic without Hegel's absolute, final denouement at the end.

This academic discourse carries the nature of Martin's transformation. Through much of his life, he saw himself alternately as a little child waiting to be fed the truth from on high and as an angry adolescent having to win the truth through battle. He became enraged at himself and his discipline when literature neither fed him the final truth nor yielded it to him after the most ferocious intellectual warfare. Thus the pattern that dominated his childhood was played out in his work and in the therapeutic relationship when he transferred onto me the expectation that I would give him the truth about his condition and the anger when I did not.

The therapeutic relationship broke that pattern. In the transference he learned that neither the therapist nor the novel nor his colleagues nor the universe had to be seen as his opponent. He realized there were a variety of ways of relating to me, to literature, and to the cosmos other than opposition born of his feeling distanced and shut out. And as his feelings about me and the other objects in his life (novels, colleagues, and so on) changed, his way of conceiving of them and relating to them changed as well. They no longer had to be cold, unresponsive objects; rather they were people and things who could be understood and related to in a wide variety of ways. Thus the increasing depth and complexity of the transference reverberated through his relations with books, colleagues, work, and his view of the world. This way of conceptualizing the therapeutic use of the transference seems most compatible with Gill's model of "analyzing the transference" by pointing out and altering patterns of interaction in the "here and now" (Gill 1979).

Two things follow from the suggestion that both the therapeutic transference and the bond with the sacred can be conceptualized as expressions of a person's internalized affective relationships. First, changes in the therapeutic transference ought to be paralleled by transformations in a person's religious experience. The previous chapter presented four cases suggestive of that possibility, tracing in some detail the congruence between transferential and religious transformations. Second, modifications of the interior world should be reflected in the experience of God. This chapter has offered several models for understanding the process by which a person's inner object world is modified and how this might affect his or her bond with the sacred. Taken together these two chapters illustrate some of the interpretive gain that might be realized in the psychoanalytic study of religion by concentrating on a person's felt bond with the sacred and conceptualizing that bond as a reflection of their inner object world and by listening through that bond for echoes of internalized affective patterns of relationship.

CHAPTER

# 5

## TOWARD A
## PSYCHOANALYSIS
## OF THE SACRED

The previous chapters began with the individual's psychodynamics, as revealed in therapy and particularly in the transference, and proposed that changes in those dynamics would be reflected in transformations in the patient's relation to the sacred. Earlier I suggested the possibility of beginning from the other side—with the person's sense of the sacred being reflected in their inner object world as well as reflecting it.

The previous analyses tacitly assume that the sense of the sacred is the dependent variable and the inner object-relational constellation is the independent variable. Assuming the priority of the psychodynamic is the only way that a strict psychoanalysis of religion can proceed. Thus we could end this study at this point. I have suggested a reenvisioning of the psychoanalysis of religion using contemporary models of transference as the primary category and have illustrated how that might proceed and what light might be shed on the psychological understanding of religion.

But there is a further implication in these newer models of transference that should not be overlooked. The claim that a strict psychoanalysis of religion must begin by assuming the primacy of psychodynamics (the way Freud, for example, did) and must consider the sacred as dependent upon them flows inevitably from the image of linear causality in which psychoanalysis, like all pre-twentieth-century science, was cast. The same image is at work in Freud's model of the transference as the projection of the patient's dynamics onto the analyst in a linear manner so that the transference is framed as totally dependent on the patient's inner conflicts.

The newer models of transference, on which this study draws, reject that linear imagery and substitute for it the image of reciprocal interaction in which neither the patient nor the analyst is primary but rather the relationship between them is. Winnicott's epigram "There is no such thing as a baby" stands for a major epistemological shift that has profound implications not only for the categories with which psychoanalysis approaches religion (substituting newer models of transference for Freud's) but, more significantly, for the very definition of the psychoanalytic approach itself. If we no longer think in terms of projections causally dependent upon inner dynamics, what happens, even within psychoanalysis, to the insistence that the sacred must be treated only as a dependent variable? Analyzing a network of interactions can start from any of the partners in the interaction or from the relationship between them. The choice of starting place is purely heuristic.

For example:

1. In the psychoanalytic relationship, as we have seen, we can look at the patient and see how his reactions to the analyst express his inner dynamics (the position Freud took). Or we can look at the analyst and see her contribution to the interaction. Or we can focus on the interaction itself (which I gather is what Gill [1979] recommends). None has a necessary priority.

2. In treating a couple or a family, one can start with the husband and see the conflicts between them as a result of, say, his passivity. Or one can start with the wife and see the conflicts between them as the result of her screaming. Or his passivity and her screaming can be viewed as a mutually reciprocal system of interaction. The choice is purely pragmatic in terms of where an intervention will be most effective (for further discussion, see Hoffman 1981).

3. In high-energy physics in which an interaction between two particles is under investigation, one can focus on the characteristics of the

individual particles (charge, spin, mass, and so on), or one can treat them as segments of an ongoing system of matter-energy interaction. The choice again is purely heuristic.

Similarly, in the psychoanalytic investigation of religion, exchanging a model of linear causality for one of reciprocal interaction, an atomistic model for a systemic one, opens up the possibility of starting the psychoanalysis of religion with the individual's dynamics (as Freud did and Rizzuto does), with the relationship between the individual's dynamics and the sacred (as I have done here), or with simply the sacred.

There is, however, a major philosophical or conceptual problem with drawing an analogy from the therapist-patient transference or the family system or a particle interaction to the relationship of human beings and God, for the analogy assumes that the components of the system or interaction are similar. Patient and therapist or family members are persons and particles are particles (whatever that involves), but, according to the religions, the human and the divine belong to different orders of being. How then can they be envisioned as part of the same conceptual system? How can one possibly draw an analogy from relationships involving similar components to one involving radically different ones?

This would be a serious, if not fatal, objection if I were attempting to *prove* the existence of God on the basis of the experience of the sacred. My purpose, however, is not to prove the existence of a divine being but only to discuss the psychological dynamics of religious experiences. Whether such experiences can be used to construct a philosophical proof for the existence of God is beyond my scope here. For my purposes, starting with the sacred means starting with the *human experience* of the sacred.

## Rudolph Otto

I am not the first to propose beginning the study of religious phenomena with the experience of the sacred and therefore to confront the ambiguity that the phrase "starting with the sacred" really means "starting with the experience of the sacred." In 1917, Rudolph Otto published a cross-cultural study of the experience of the sacred entitled in German *Das Heilige,* which was later translated into English under the misleading title *The Idea of the Holy*—misleading because Otto's concern is not with the *idea* but with the *experience* of the holy.

Otto begins by suggesting that the experience of the holy is unique, completely unlike any other experience, and so it cannot be comprehended by philosophical or psychological categories. It is "perfectly *sui generis* and irreducible. . . . while it admits of being discussed, it cannot be strictly defined . . . [or] taught; it can only be evoked, awakened in the mind" (1958:7). Otto is not simply saying that the *holy* itself is beyond our categories and cannot be defined; he is saying that the human *experience* of the holy is also indefinable. The experience cannot be analyzed, only evoked. Hence only evocative rather than analytic language is appropriate. (A critique of Otto's position can be found in Proudfoot [1985].)

Having said this, Otto attempts a description of the experience of the holy, but not before first evoking it by asking the reader to "direct his mind to a moment of deeply felt religious experience. . . . whoever cannot do this . . . is requested to read no further" (1958:8). Otto is not trying to convince the skeptic but rather to organize an experience with which he can assume all his readers are familiar. As part of this project, he coins a Latin term—*mysterium tremendum*—which he calls the "only one appropriate expression" of the experience of the holy (1958:12). *Tremendum* refers to the uncanny, eerie sense accompanying an uncommon and unfamiliar experience. This feeling Otto takes to be the origin of religion. "Emerging in the mind of primeval man, [it] forms the starting-point for the entire religious development in history. . . . this fact of our nature—primary, unique, underivable from anything else—[is] the basic factor and the basic impulse underlying the entire process of religious evolution" (1958:13). The other fundamental characteristic of the experience of the holy is *mysterium,* which refers to the holy being so far beyond our comprehension that it fills "the mind with blank wonder and astonishment" (1958:27). Struck dumb before the mystery of the holy, the mind can only conclude that the sacred is, in a term that occurs over and over in *Das Heilige,* "wholly other" (1958:23–29).

Otto insists that the feeling of mysterium tremendum is not simply a deepening or intensifying of ordinary emotions. The experience of the holy is not on a continuum with other human experiences but is rather sui generis. In support of this claim, Otto appeals to direct experience rather than to argument. In speaking about the tremendum, he writes, "any one who is capable of more precise introspection must recognize that the distinction between such a 'dread' and natural fear is not simply one of degree of intensity" (1958:15). The wholly otherness of God is reflected in the wholly otherness of the experience of God, the absolute gulf between God and humankind paralleled by the absolute gulf between the experience of the holy and other experiences.

Otto attributes absolute transcendence to God ("wholly other") not on the basis of theological or philosophical argument but on the basis of emotional experience. Because the experience of the sacred evokes feelings of awe, dread, incomprehension, and mystery in us, the object of that experience must be mysterious and beyond comprehension. Here Otto gets into trouble when he writes, "the truly 'mysterious' object is beyond our apprehension and comprehension, not only because our knowledge has certain irremovable limits, but because in it we come upon something inherently 'wholly other,' whose kind and character are incommensurable with our own" (1958:28). To Otto, the concept of God as "wholly other" is not a concept at all but a datum of experience. We experience the fact that God is beyond experience.

Surely this will not do. We cannot be said to experience that something is beyond experience. Starting with God, the wholly other, can only mean starting with the experience of God whose otherness is not beyond our experience but is rather a part of our experience. The point is that characteristics of the experience of an object are not necessarily characteristics of the object. In a dark room at night I may experience a noise as frightening. When I turn a light on and discover the wind is blowing the screen door open and closed, the experience of the noise ceases to be frightening. The noise in itself was neither frightening nor not frightening. My *experience* of the noise in a dark room was. Scariness is a characteristic not of the noise but only of my experience of it in a certain context. The fact that our experience of God has a numinous, mysterious, wholly other quality does not mean that God is wholly other. But it does suggest that an adequate psychology of religion should offer an account of where that numinous quality of the experience of the sacred comes from.

What Otto might be pointing to with the use of terms like "perfectly *sui generis* and irreducible . . . and absolutely primary and elementary" is that the sacred evokes what is primary and fundamental *in our experience*. Psychologically, then, to start with the sacred means to start with the psyche's most fundamental experiences: those constituting its creation and re-creation. The quality of sacredness refers to the potential to resonate with the deepest recesses of ourselves. What makes the experience of the holy mysterium tremendum is that it reverberates with the awesomeness and mystery of the depths of selfhood. In that sense the experience of the sacred is "absolutely primary and elementary."

## Christopher Bollas

In a series of reflections on psychoanalysis provocatively titled (in a phrase taken from Freud) *The Shadow of the Object,* a psychoanalyst and professor of literature, Christopher Bollas, struggles with many of the same issues regarding the deep structure of psychotherapeutic change discussed in the previous chapter, covering the same ground in different terminology. In the process, he makes some important observations about the psychology of the sacred. Bollas takes as the theme of his essays "the human subject's recording of his early experiences of the object. This is the shadow of the object as it falls on the ego, leaving some trace of its existence in the adult" (1987:3).

Bollas is reaching back to the earliest days of awareness, to the child's most primal and foundational sensibilities. Following Winnicott, Bollas identifies the content of this primary consciousness as the child-mother dyad and recognizes that our first awareness is not of an object but of a relationship, for "the rhythms of this process . . . inform the nature of this 'object' relation rather than the qualities of the object as object. Not yet fully identified as an other, the mother is experienced as a process" (1987:14). It is this *relationship* between herself and the caregiver that the infant internalizes, for "the baby does not internalize an object, but . . . a process derived from an object" (1987:50).

The child when grown may play out the internalized relationship in ways discussed in earlier chapters of this book, scripting herself or parts of herself and others into the various roles. "Each person transfers elements of the parents' child care to his own handling of himself as object," Bollas writes. "In that transference to the self as an object, the person represents the interplay of the inherited (true self) and the environmental" (1987:59). Like other authors surveyed in this book, Bollas concentrates on current feelings and behavior as re-creations of the internalized infantile interpersonal environment. And his focus falls more on the affective tone of those internalizations and re-creations than on patterns of action and behavior.

This comes out in his discussion of "moods," which are "complex self states that may establish a mnemic [one that stores something of the past in memory] environment in which the individual re-experiences and re-creates former infant-child experiences and states of being" (1987:102). Thus, "when a person goes into a mood, he may be some former self" (1987:100). Most likely he becomes someone he knew himself to be in childhood: a guilty party, a shameful wrongdoer, a klutz, a grandiose object of admiration, a neglected object, an elated conqueror. Or sometimes, if opportunities for experiencing himself were severely constricted in growing up, "when a person goes 'into' a mood, he becomes that child self who was refused expression in relation to his parents" (1987:115).

The kernel of a mood Bollas calls a "conservative object," using "object" in the now familiar sense of a dyadic or interpersonal experience. Such a state is called "conservative" because it conserves a childhood experience of self or other or a childhood psychological state that is "preserved intact within a person's internal world: it is not intended to change, and acts as a mnemic container of a particular self state conserved because it is linked to the child self's continuing negotiation with some aspect of the early parental environment" (1987:110).

Thus, the inner world is not simply a world of internalized objects, images, and representations. Bollas emphasizes a theme stressed throughout this book: the inner world is also a world of internalized interpersonally generated affects, feelings, and moods.

> A child not only stores his experiences of an object in that process we term internalization, but he also conserves self states which may eventually become permanent features of his character. Furthermore, the internal world is not simply composed of self and object representations. . . . A child may endure an experience which is registered not through object

representation but through an identity sense. . . . A child may thus have a profound self experience without being able to link this being state to any one object. Such self states are nonetheless untranslatable into that symbolic order characteristic of object representation: they yield, instead, identity senses and they therefore conserve the child's sense of self or sense of being (1987:110).

This is particularly true of traumatic events that, by definition, overwhelm the child's immature capacities for symbolization, representation, and therefore integration. Such events are even more likely than others to live on in the inner world in an unintegrated, "conservative," condition. Bollas points to episodes in which "a child may undergo an intensely private self experience that defies his representative capacity, so that the being state persists as a conserved rather than a transformed (symbolized) phenomenon" (1987:111). For Bollas this is especially true of those traumas that represent a failure in parenting through neglect, abuse, excessive harshness, or lack of empathy. He virtually restricts the genesis of moods (at least negative ones, which is all he really treats) to deficiencies in the parent-child dyad when he writes, "a conservative object preserves the child's relation to the parents at the moment of a breakdown in parent-child engagement" (1987:113).

Another reason such states persist, besides their being unmanageable for a child, is that they serve to preserve the child's relationship to her parents. No matter how painful they may be, such states and the moods they generate carry a sense of continuity from the adult back to her childhood. One might think patients would readily abandon such painful and troublesome affects. But Bollas notes a phenomenon familiar in the clinical arena—patients in therapy often resist the passing of such states not because they are obstinate but because they "feel the analyst is endeavouring to remove the preserved relationship to the parents" (1987:113). This function of moods is especially important if such conservative objects arise primarily at times of fracture in the parent-child relationship. Those are the times when it would be particularly important for the child to try to preserve whatever she felt remained of her relationship to the parent. The child might freeze such a moment in memory.

Since we are dealing with experiences occurring before the dawn of discursive thought, they are recorded not in words or mental representations but in more diffuse and affective sensibilities. "The object can cast its shadow without a child being able to process this relation through mental representations or language," Bollas notes, "as, for example, when a parent uses his child to contain projective identifications. While we do know something of the character of the object which affects us, we may not have thought it yet" (1987:3). These primal "senses" are the "unthought known"; they constitute the focus of his reflections and represent a knowing prior to speaking.

All later feelings about self and world are built upon the experience of the mother-child dyad. This relational matrix provides the catalyst for integrating experiences (bodily sensations; primitive sights, smells, and sounds; pains and pleasures; the precursors of thought) into a sense of self and other. Thus Bollas terms this most primary maternal milieu the "transformational object" (I think it would be clearer to call it the "transformational object relationship") because in it the child learns to transform experience into information about self and world.

> I wish to identify the infant's first subjective experience of the object as a transformational object and . . . address the trace in adult life of this early relationship. It is an identification that emerges from symbiotic relating, where the first object is "known" not so much by putting it into object representation but as a recurrent experience of being—a more existential as opposed to representational knowing. . . . the mother helps to integrate the infant's being (instinctual, cognitive, affective, environmental). . . . the mother is experienced as a process of transformation. (1987:14)

Bollas is clearly pointing to a phenomenon similar to Kohut's selfobject, a relationship crucial for the development and maintenance of a sense of self. At first the infant is dependent upon the other for comfort, food, security, and so on. Later these capacities are integrated and taken over by the infant himself.

So potent is this primary transformational tie to the mother that it casts a long shadow extending throughout a person's life. In times of crisis, the person longs for a transformational object who can comfort and facilitate the integration of new experience. In moments of ecstasy, what Bollas calls "the aesthetic," a new transformational object has been discovered in another person, or an overpowering piece of music, or an evocative poem or novel, or the awesomeness of nature. Not only in these transformational moments but throughout all of life the search for the lost transformational object goes on.

> This feature of early existence lives on in certain forms of object seeking in adult life. . . . the quest is not to possess the object; rather the object is pursued in order to surrender to it as a medium that alters the self, where the subject-as-supplicant now feels himself to be the recipient of envirosomtic caring, identified with metamorphosis of the self. . . . The memory of this early object relation manifests itself in the person's search for an object (a person, place, event, ideology) that promises to transform the self. (1987:14)

Although similar in some ways to Winnicott's notion of the transitional object and Kohut's image of object seeking as object hunger, there is an important difference as well. For Bollas the transformational object is never simply put aside. The transformational object may itself be transformed (from the maternal matrix into "a person, place, event, or ideology"), but it is not outgrown. Of course, as I noted earlier, for Winnicott the transitional *object* is put aside but the transitional *capacity* to experience in an imaginative and fruitful way continues to mature and develop. In this sense Bollas's transformational object and Winnicott's transitional phenomenon are similar: both point to the creative capacity lying at the heart of both art and science.

I noted in my earlier discussion of Rizzuto some of the limitations on the religious appropriation of the idea of the transitional object and it would seem that Bollas's concept of a transformational object might be closer to the reality of religious experience since, like the experience of God, it is precisely something that is transformed (as Rizzuto herself documents in relation to the image of God) and not necessarily disposed of.

While Kohut clearly insists that we never outgrow the need for selfobjects to sustain us, he sometimes sounds like the search for selfobjects to transform us is rooted in developmental deficiencies and represents a form of object hunger to make up for undeveloped self-structures and self-capacities. Presumably such object hunger is to be outgrown as developmental arrests are overcome and new self-structures are grown. On the other hand, for Bollas, since the search for a transformational object is rooted not in deficiency but in the positive experience of the caretaking dyad, it represents neither an emptiness nor a lack of self-structure but rather the natural desire to recover and reexperience something positive and growth enhancing. The ecstasy of romance, aesthetics, and religion become the potentially positive carriers of this necessary aspect of human experience.

> In adult life, therefore, to seek the transformational object is to recollect an early object experience, to remember not cognitively but existentially—through intense affective experience—a relationship which was identified with cumulative transformational experiences of the self. Its intensity as an object relation is not due to the fact that this is an object of desire but to the object being identified with such powerful metamorphoses of being. In the aesthetic moment the subject briefly re-experiences, through ego fusion with the aesthetic object, a sense of the subjective attitude towards the transformational object. (1987:17)

Such a theory leads inevitably to a psychology of the sacred. Bollas's discussion of the transformational object stands in the tradition of Otto's insistence on the primacy of the sacred. For Otto the sacred was not a concept, trait, or entity but rather a type of experience that was overpowering, awe inspiring, compelling, and inexhaustible. Such a way of thinking about the sacred—as a characteristic of certain experiences—carries some obvious links to Bollas's discussion of the transformational object. Bollas himself clearly sees these links when he writes, "the anticipation of being transformed by an object . . . inspires the subject with a reverential attitude towards it. . . . the adult subject tends to nominate such objects as sacred" (1987:16–17).

The encounter with the holy continues the self's fundamental experience of being constituted as a self in the psychological womb of the transforming object. The power of the sacred is, in part, that it carries the potential of recapturing the psyche's moment of creation and with it the promise of present and future moments of re-creation. Bollas begins his book with the discussion of the transforming object. Consciously or not, this structural point reflects a deeper one—the primacy of the transforming object in the psychological birth (and rebirth) of the person. This, in turn, echoes Otto's insistence on the primacy of the holy.

Such a psychology of the sacred has several important implications for the psychological study of religion.

First, it implies that encounters with the sacred are almost inevitably experiences of transformation. Experiences of the sacred carry us back and put us in touch with the foundations of our being and knowing—the transformational object. "Aesthetic moments do not sponsor memories of a specific event or relationship," Bollas suggests, "but evoke a psychosomatic sense of fusion that is the subject's recollection of the transformational object" (1987:16). Such transforming moments are not re-creations or memories of past events but rather represent a return to the foundational experiences of human life. Such a return to the wellspring of our conscious existence carries the hope and the possibility of metamorphosis, of reworking or transforming aspects of ourselves and our relation to the world.

Are such experiences regressive? It depends on the connotation of the term *regressive*. Such experiences—whether found through art, religion, romance, nature, or wherever—represent a return to a more primal (perhaps the most primal) state of consciousness. But they also make possible the jump forward to new levels of integration and transformation by re-creating the milieu that is the psychological catalyst of transformation.

Second, by rooting the experience of the sacred in the most basic of human dynamics, Bollas implies (like Otto) that we are all *homo religiosis* (inherently religious); we all have the potential for transformative sacred experiences. The search for the transformational object or experience is not a neurotic response to the threat of instinctual forces but rather a continuation of the primary experience that constitutes and reconstitutes the self. It is an expression of our basic personhood and is found in many domains of human existence.

> We have failed to take notice of the phenomenon in adult life of the wide-ranging collective search for an object that is identified with the metamorphosis of the self. In many religious faiths, for example, when the subject believes in the deity's actual potential to transform the total environment, he sustains the terms of the earliest object tie within a mythic

structure. In secular worlds, we see how hope invested in various objects (a new job, a move to another country, a vacation, a change of relationship) may both represent a request for a transformational experience and, at the same time, continue the "relationship" to an object that signifies the experience of transformation. We know that the advertising world makes its living on the trace of this object. (1987:16)

Not a regression to an infantile state, the search for transformation is rather a part of the ongoing process of human development. All of us have the drive to reexperience the moment of psychic creation and the process of metamorphosis. But we were not created in isolation and so the need for growth and change drives for a transforming *object-relation* that will sponsor that change.

The third implication derives inevitably from the previous one. Bollas is aware that an intrinsic drive for the transforming object relation can take negative and destructive as well as positive forms (1987:17). The ubiquity and necessity of transformational objects mean that this impulse must go somewhere, as the previous quote illustrates. This psychological observation—that "hope [is] invested in various objects (a new job, a move to another country, a vacation, a change of relationship) . . . [and] the advertising world makes its living on the trace of this object" (1987:16)—echoes a concern of many contemporary theologians—idolatry.

Even before the advent of modern theology or psychology, Friedrich Nietzsche noted that, though God is dead, men must have gods and so will make gods of the state, the party, or whatever suits them. Any suggestion that humankind is *homo religiosis* and that the drive for the sacred, or its source, does not lie in curable defenses or neuroses but is as intrinsic to human nature as sexuality or interpersonal relations entails that this drive will latch onto one object or another without regard to whether the object can bear the full weight and range of the experience of the holy or fulfill all social and psychological functions of the sacred.

It was Søren Kierkegaard who first cast this essentially religious diagnosis of the human condition in primarily psychological terms. Kierkegaard (1941) saw human consciousness passing through three stages. First was the aesthetic, the search for pleasure that drives for repetition as we seek to reexperience pleasure. But repetition leads to boredom, for even the most intense pleasures turn stale after a while. At first the aesthete deals with the staleness of one pleasure by going on to another, and then another. But if he is at all self-reflective, eventually the experience of boredom will call the whole search for pleasure into question.

The person then moves on to the ethical stage where he seeks meaning in life through committing himself to something outside of himself. At first he gives himself wholeheartedly to his new ideal, but eventually he falls short of its demands, and so the ethical leads inevitably to a realization of human finitude and failure, if not to guilt and despair. And so the ethical, rather than bringing meaning to life, results in a new level of pain. The person is still inwardly divided, for he is looking to something outside of the self to give meaning to life. At this point, the person can give up the search (a process Kierkegaard calls "resignation") and, thrown back on himself by the failure of the ethical stage, find the divine within.

Kierkegaard's image of human development as a process of trying unsuccessfully to wring meaning from finite experiences (pleasure, duty, effort) until all finite experiences fail and one is brought face to face with the infinite is behind contemporary theology's concern with "idolatry," which another twentieth-century theologian, Reinhold Niebuhr, called "absolutizing the relative." In Bollas's language, an idol would be an object that claims to be transformative but is only partially so or is destructively transformative. It evokes and plays on our longing for transformations but cannot deliver on the promise. In Kierkegaardian terms, Bollas describes the search for the transforming object without raising the theological question of whether any or all such finite objects can in fact be more than partially and temporarily transformative.

Bollas's discussion of the transformative object, the reverberation of our deepest and most primal object relationship, is also a psychology of the sacred. The primacy of the transforming object parallels Otto's insistence on the primacy of the experience of the holy. On the surface it might appear, though, as if these models point in opposite directions: Otto's toward the sacred as transcendent (wholly other) and Bollas's toward the sacred as immanent (found in the depths of our inner world). But we have seen that Otto's insistence that we experience God as wholly other is misleading. We cannot, within human experience, encounter what is intrinsically beyond human experience. Otto is right to insist that the experience of the sacred is numinous and mysterious but possibly wrong to attribute that to the sacred, as experienced, dwelling beyond experience. Rather this numinosity might arise from some other source.

One possibility, suggested by Bollas, is that the quality of numinosity comes from the ability to transform us by reevoking the birth of the self, that primal transformation of experience into self-structure through the dyadic catalyst of the transforming object. Thus the experience of the sacred is inevitably the experience of a transforming relationship. The languages of transcendence and immanence meet in the encounter with a transforming object. The experience of the sacred has a transcendental, numinous quality not because the sacred is a wholly other object but because such experiences resonate with the primal originating depths of selfhood.

## Paul Tillich

Something is denoted as sacred, then, if it evokes the matrix out of which the self originates. The same theme echoes in the work of the twentieth-century philosopher and theologian Paul Tillich. As we saw with Otto, there is no escaping the confines of human experience, even when speaking of the transcendent. The experience of the transcendent always begins from, or occurs in conjunction with, some human experience. For Otto it was the experience of being overwhelmed and awe-struck; for Bollas it was the experience of transformation; for Tillich it is an experience he calls "ontic shock." The term *ontic* and its kin *ontological* come from the Greek word for "being" or "existence." Ontic shock is the question of existence, of why things exist, of why there is something and not nothing. (The following discussion is based primarily on Tillich [1951].)

Such a question is easy to satirize in a Woody Allen way, but Tillich points out that the same question can be asked from two standpoints and mean two different things. Abstractly I can wonder, why is anything here? What is the meaning of existence? Or, more personally, I can cry out, why am I here? What, if anything, is the meaning of my life? The first question is the basis of philosophy; the second Tillich calls the basis of religion that concerns itself not with the general question of the origin of the universe or the human species but rather with the personal question of the possible source and significance of one's own life. This question is not voiced with detachment; rather, the individual has a profound stake in the answer.

The ultimate heuristic origin of all these questions, Tillich says, is the experiential shock of existence itself, the mystery that anything exists rather than there being chaos or nothingness. And, although Tillich doesn't mention it, there is the further shock of realizing the improbability of there being existences aware of their existence: creatures able to recognize that they exist and to be awed by it.

What, then, does it mean to exist? The word *existence* comes from two Greek words *ek-ist,* meaning "to stand out from." Stand out from what? Nonexistence, Tillich answers. To exist is to overcome the threat of nonexistence. *Existence* in this sense is a verb, not a noun; a process, not a static state. These semantic observations carry an important psychological message: existence is precarious, always shadowed by the possibility of ceasing to exist, the threat of not being. Thus anxiety is inevitable (it was Tillich who coined the phrase for his epoch as the "age of anxiety"). Such necessary anxiety Tillich calls "ontological," for it is woven into the fabric of existence and no psychotherapy can remove it. Such anxiety is distinguished from what Tillich calls "neurotic anxiety," which is a function of a person's history and can be therapeutically remedied (Tillich 1952).

Existence, the overcoming of the threat of not-being, is possible, Tillich reasons, only because there is a power or force of being that keeps the threat of not-being at bay and sustains everything in existence. Things exist because this possibility of nonexistence is overcome by a power or force Tillich calls the "power of being" or "being itself." This power is what men and women call God.

God, for Tillich, is the source of existence, the "ground of being," the power of existing itself. *Being,* for Tillich, is a verb, not a noun; it is the activity of overcoming the possibility of not-being and of sustaining in existence everything from the basic particles of physics to the furthest reaches of the curved universe. God is the ultimate answer to the question of why there is something rather than nothing—an answer not in terms of the symmetries and forces of natural science but rather in terms of the source of those primary laws and structures themselves.

Although sustained by the power of being, everything that exists is contingent, dogged by the shadow of possible nonexistence. We can imagine the world without trees, without animals, even without homo sapiens. We know there was time before we existed and time when we will cease to be. Through the paradoxes of physics we can envision other worlds, other universes, built from other types of particles and obeying other laws. None of this is necessary or inevitable.

Existence therefore means contingency, finitude, precariousness, and thus, for those who are conscious, inevitable anxiety. To exist, then, is to be dependent, to depend upon the power of being. None of this applies to God. Thus Tillich reasons that it is mistaken to say that God exists. He is not denying that there is an ultimate reality; rather, he is denying that the predicate *existence* can be applied to God. The term *existence* cannot be meaningfully applied to God, for it makes little sense to say that existence exists. Because God transcends the limits of finite existence, none of the terms drawn from within those limits—even the term *existence* itself—applies to God. The only existence we know is limited, dependent, and transitory, but God is none of these.

For Tillich, we must begin with God, for God is the beginning of everything. The power of existing makes everything else possible. God alone was, as the Torah says, "in the beginning." The known world remains absolutely dependent on God to keep it from utter nothingness. That is the meaning of the term *God*. To experience God, then, is to move from the experience of ontological shock—the dread that comes when we confront the precariousness of life—to the realization of the power of being itself, the experience of the source that sustains existence in the face of nothingness and provides the basis for the courage to live in the face of life's inevitable uncertainty.

## Martin Buber

Otto elided two references of the term *holy:* the holy as a transcendent object, the wholly other, and the holy as a characteristic of experience—numinosity, mysteriousness—which can apply to our encounter with objects within our world, objects we usually call holy. The failure to distinguish carefully between these two meanings of the term *holy* creates a certain amount of philosophical confusion in Otto's work, but it may make some psychological sense. There may be a psychological, if not a logical, connection between the stance we take toward the objects in our world and the possibility of encountering the transcendent in and through them. The capacity to experience certain objects-in-relation as holy may be the psychological precondition of an object relation with the holy. It was not a psychologist but a philosopher, Martin Buber, who most powerfully explored the connection between ordinary experience and the experience of God. (The following discussion is based on Buber [1970, pts. I and III].)

There are, according to Buber, two stances we can take toward the objects of our experience: the "I-it" stance and the "I-you" stance. The semantic structure of this distinction might lead one to think that Buber was dividing the world into two classes—"yous" and "its," persons and stones. In fact, Buber is doing exactly the reverse. The difference between the "I-you" and the "I-it" is not the object but the "I"—I am different in an "I-you" and an "I-it" relationship. In the "I-it," I keep myself aloof, detached, uninvolved. I see the other as a means of achieving my predetermined goal. In the "I-you," I am involved, caring, committed. I respect the other's freedom and autonomy.

Since the difference lies not in the object but in the stance I take toward the object, I can have a "youish" or an "itish" relationship with any object. (In years of teaching Buber, I have not found an adequate way of translating his approach into descriptive language; the best I have been able to do is to use the circumlocution of "youish" and "itish" as adjectives describing the two basic relational stances.) The example Buber uses is the scientist and the poet facing a tree. The scientist approaches the tree "itishly": she takes the attitude of a detached observer. The tree is an object of scrutiny and study, to be categorized and fit within some theoretical framework. Allowed no integrity of its own, the tree is treated as part of a general zoological class. The poet, on the other hand, involves himself with the tree (one might think of the painter Monet immersing himself in the experience of the lily pond in preparation for painting *Waterlilies*). The goal of the artist's relationship is not to classify the tree or sublate it into a general biological theory but to allow it to stand as a unique object. The object—the tree—is the same. The difference is in the ways the scientist and the poet interact with it, each stance giving rise to different kinds of information.

Buber is not a romantic or a moralist insisting that all relationships should be of the "youish" type. I may have only an instrumental relationship with, say, the attendant at the gas station. We meet briefly only as functionaries: he fills the tank of my car and I give him money. There is nothing wrong with that. The problem comes, Buber says, when we become so involved in the "I-it" world that we lose the capacity ever to relate "youishly."

To speak of losing the capacity for "youish" relationships implies that we all once had it. For Buber, the "I-you' is the primary mode of relationship. Our most basic stance on the world is "youish." It is the way of the child; to the child, the teddy bear is a true friend. Birthday parties are thrown for him, he is named and hugged, and consulted on the weighty matters of childhood. And not just children. Race car drivers name their cars. They talk them out of tight spaces and around dangerous curves. They lovingly polish that cage of metal on which, for a few moments, their lives depend. The alcoholic sings to the bottle, rages at it, mourns its passing, and brightens at its return. We personify what we are most intimately connected with. Personifying is our most fundamental mode—it is what makes us human. When we lose the capacity to personify, to, as Buber says, "speak the primary word you," when we relate even to those most intimate to us in a detached way and seem them only as a means to getting what we want, we have lost part of our humanity.

The exception to the rule that anything can be related to as "you" or "it" is God. Buber calls God the "eternal you" by which he means God is eternally you. Buber's central theological maxim is that "the eternal You cannot become an It" (1970:160). This is not so much a statement about God as about our relationship to God. God can be approached only "youishly." To deal with God from a detached or invulnerable position is to relate not to God at all but only to an idol, a finite thing put in the place of God—a concept, an abstract principle, a transitory feeling. Thus philosophy and theology, no matter how pious, become for Buber the first step toward atheism, for they approach God as an idea or concept rather than as a personal presence who can only be encountered.

Only when we relate to others "youishly" can we encounter God in the heart of those "youish" relationships. A pious student pours over a sacred text day after day. Suddenly the words that have been read hundreds of times before strike her in a new way and the text comes alive. The text has not changed, but her relationship to the text has. And in that moment, she meets the eternal you through that "youish" encounter with the print and page. Two friends have known each other for years. Suddenly he says something and his friend sees him differently and the relationship changes. In that moment of transformation and newfound intimacy the presence of God might be glimpsed. Some climbers ascend a mountain and spend the night there. They awaken on the summit awestruck by the vista of autumn colors refracting the dawning hues of the new day. In that "aesthetic" (in Bollas's sense) instant, something of the eternal might be glimpsed through the glowing kaleidoscope of the sunrise.

The spread of atheism, then, represents not the decline of the intellectual credibility of religion but rather the decline of the psychological capacity to relate to the world in a "youish" way and to see through all our "youish" encounters to the "eternal you" who stands behind them.

In ways clearly congruent with the object-relational framework articulated in this book, Buber begins from the primacy of the self in relationship. For him, the isolated self is an abstraction and the only realistic starting point for understanding human behavior and human consciousness is the interpersonal self. Kohut represents a consistent application of this perspective to psychopathology and psychotherapy; Buber represents its consistent application to the field of religion: just as the self comes to know itself only as a partner in dialogue, so God becomes known only as a partner in dialogue. (More on these points can be found in Smith [1985], a nuanced and creative exploration of Buber and Kohut.)

## A Psychology of the Sacred

For Tillich, what is sacred is what is universal, the power of being itself. For Buber, on the other hand, what is sacred is what is most personal, the "eternal you" encountered through our most profound intimacies. Whereas Tillich is suspicious of personifying and calls the image of a personal God "a confusing symbol" (1951:245), Buber thinks there is no other way to approach the sacred. The term *God* is holy, he says, not because it is used to speak *of* God but because it is used to speak *to* him (1970:123).

The split between Tillich and Buber over the primacy of personal or impersonal categories for the sacred mirrors other splits in modernity: the Cartesian split of subject and object, the cultural split of public and private domains (Jones 1982). Psychoanalysis, particularly Kohut's self psychology, might suggest that these splits reflect a split within the psyche whereby the living personal core of the self is split off and the person has access only to the more impersonal aspects of herself. This could be a Kohutian way of making Buber's point about the loss of the capacity in modern culture to speak the primary word "you" to others (and to ourselves).

Kohut and Buber, from very different perspectives, suggest that there are not two classes of objects—personal and impersonal. We make the objects of our object relations personal or impersonal by the stance we take: by being "youish" or "itish" in relation to them, by being open to them as selfobjects or keeping them at a distance. Beyond that, Bollas speaks of "the self as object" (1987:41ff.), suggesting that the same dynamics that govern all object relations also apply to ourselves. We can approach ourself impersonally or "itishly." This is reflected in the clinical phenomenon of people who describe themselves as though they were talking about a third person. Unlike the profoundly schizoid person, such patients do not speak of themselves in the language of the third person (calling themselves "he" or "she" instead of "I"), but they narrate their life stories in such an abstract way that it feels like a story about someone else.

This principle—that nothing is intrinsically personal or impersonal— also applies to our bond with the sacred. Whether the sacred is discussed in personal or impersonal categories depends on the stance we take. From this standpoint, the tension between personal and impersonal languages for God is not a contradiction to be resolved. Rather, these differing theologies result from different stances toward the sacred or the establishment of a different kind of selfobject relationship.

Impersonal images of the sacred (as energy, force, the ground of being) can be bearers of an intense, passionate, and lasting bond with the sacred. This was apparently the case, for example, with Tillich, who thought of God in abstract philosophical terms but could speak of God and religious experience with passion and conviction (anyone who doubts this should read his collections of sermons, *The New Being* and *The Shaking of the Foundations,* as well as his autobiography *On the Boundary*). My patient Barbara, described previously, ended treatment with an image of God as a creative life force—on the surface a more impersonal metaphor than her earlier image of God the companion but one that functioned in a more psychologically compelling way.

In the language of Kohut and Bollas, an impersonal concept of God can perform a profound and personal selfobject or transforming function in an individual's psychological economy. Certain ways of speaking about the sacred may employ impersonal philosophical or even scientific categories, but the bond established with them and through them may be profoundly personal and affectively powerful.

Another implication of this principle that nothing is intrinsically personal or impersonal is that a book, an idea, a tree, can (in Kohut's terms) be a selfobject, our relation to it central to who we are, if we are open to being nourished and encountered by it, or, as Buber would say, if we can approach it in a "youish" way. For Bollas, too, the transforming object can be a physical thing or a mental representation. Thus there have been and continue to be sacred books, sacred ideas, sacred trees.

Part of the psychology of the sacred, then, is to account for the experience of the sacredness of otherwise ordinary ideas, objects, and events. In their own ways Kohut, Buber, and Bollas point to some of the dynamics involved when family meals, groves of trees, cups and plates, mountain peaks, items of clothing, books and scrolls, ideas, gestures, and the full range of human activities become designated as holy and become the means through which a passionate bond with the sacred is established. For this is what the religious life of human beings usually consists of: encountering the transforming and sustaining source of selfhood through holy words and books, evocative rituals and gestures, compelling ideas and powerful communities, the glories of nature, or an encounter with the depths of the self.

For Otto, sacredness resides in the experiential qualities of awesomeness and mystery, giving the sacred a feeling of being wholly other. Winnicott implies that the sacred is encountered through a transitional state of awareness transcending subjectivity and objectivity. Bollas suggests that sacredness consists in transformative power, the capacity to evoke the foundations of selfhood. Tillich also defines the sacred as the power of origination, the origination not just of the self but of the entire universe. For all his abstract language, Tillich's primary concern, too, is with the *experience* of the sacred. To experience God is to encounter the power that keeps all things in being, an encounter that comes through facing our finitude—anxiety, suffering, meaninglessness, precariousness, and other masks worn by the threat of nonbeing.

That this experience of the sacred is structured by psychological processes arising from the depths of selfhood is an idea found in both Bollas and Loewald. For Bollas, the unconscious is built around an experience of transformation; for Loewald, the unconscious brings with it a sense of timelessness and unity. Experiences engaging us at the depths of our selfhood will be accompanied by perceptions of unity and timelessness and perhaps be times of transformation.

For Loewald, human life is impoverished if deprived of access to what he calls "the primary level of mentation." Re-immersion in the primary process through moments of rapture and ecstasy is necessary for psychic refreshment and rejuvenation; it is the source of creativity, sanity, and a fully human life, since "the range and richness of human life is directly proportional to the mutual responsiveness between these various mental phases and levels" (1978:61). This, of course, echoes Winnicott's concern for "the creative living first manifest in play" (1971:100).

Winnicott's schema is more linear. The capacity for play develops into creativity in the arts and sciences, but in the process it seems that playing per se is left behind. Loewald's model is more reciprocal. Primary process is never outgrown but is returned to again and again. But if Winnicott's transitional process means not only a developmental stage or the use of certain objects soon to be outgrown but also the entering of a certain transitional state of consciousness or psychological space, then Winnicott's and Loewald's theories are much closer than they first appear to be. Teddy bears and blankets are put aside, but the capacity to enter and reenter that transitional consciousness where the subject-object dualism of "objectifying mentation" (Loewald 1978:51) is transcended abides as the source of "creative living."

Loewald and Winnicott agree that one of the tasks of religion is the cultivation of this richness of consciousness. Such religious moments are transitional not only because they transcend subjectivity and objectivity (Meissner) or invoke imagination (Rizzuto) but also because they allow us to enter again and again into that timeless and transforming psychological space from which renewal and creativity emerge. And what makes such experiences continually renewing? Perhaps, as Bollas suggests, in the presence of a transforming object relationship, we gain access again to the formative (and reformative) experience at the heart of selfhood, the experience Tillich calls the power of being. According to the relational model on which this book is based, the core of selfhood is internalized interpersonal episodes (Stern's RIGS). Besides being characterized by timelessness, unity, and transformation, moments that evoke the depths of our personal being will be carried by profoundly personal metaphors, or as Buber would say, they will be "I-you" and not "I-it" encounters. Put another way, the unity that is experienced there is a unity in which selfhood is sustained, not lost.

The relational psychoanalysis of religion outlined here provides new and illuminating categories with which to investigate religion, centering around the reenactment of the patterns and affects associated with internalized and generalized object relations. It also offers a definition of human nature as intrinsically relational as opposed to the atomistic individualism of earlier psychoanalytic theory. But it goes further still when it points to those transitional psychological spaces, continually reverberating with the affects of past object relations and pregnant with the possibility of future forms of mentation (Loewald) and transformation (Bollas) that religion may evoke for us through word, ritual, or intense introspective discipline.

Kierkegaard suggested that human life, when driven to its limits, strikes God, for the Spirit is the source of the self's relation to itself. In that Kierkegaardian spirit of pushing things as far as they can go, I offer a concluding unscientific postscript to this book.

Theories of the transference are also implicitly theories of the nature of the self: the self constituted by its defenses against instincts, the self created by its inner objects, the self structured by its internalized relationships, the self generated by the organization of its experiences. Post-Freudian theories agree that the self is inherently relational. At the most superficial level, we know about ourselves only from the feedback we receive from others. At the dynamic level, our anxieties, fears, motivations, and ideals seem to be a function of the experiences we internalize from our interactions in the world. The structures of our selfhood are the transmutations of our interactions.

Theologians have known for generations that such a sense of the self as inherently related, if carried to its ultimate end, yields a strikingly religious vision. Scheiermacher's God as the "whence of our feeling of absolute dependence," H. R. Niebuhr's "God as the single power behind all the powers that impinge upon us," Tillich's "God as the ground of our being"—perhaps all these are best summed up in Buber's epigram that "all lines of relation meet in the Eternal You." The psychoanalyst asks about the object-relational sources of these various images of God. The theologian suggests that if transference is the grounding metaphor of our reality, it is not illogical to allow our reality to be transferentially grounded. If our psychology is inherently relational, it is not antipsychological to see reality as interrelated. If there is no escaping dependency on a selfobject milieu, there is nothing childish about acknowledging connection to a self-sustaining universal matrix. If selves necessarily stand in relation, it is not necessarily irrational to ask if this complex of selves in relation does not itself stand in relation.

# REFERENCES

Alexander, F. (1963). *Fundamentals of Psychoanalysis*. New York: Norton.

Allport, G. (1950). *The Individual and His Religion*. New York: Macmillan.

Aronson, H. (1985). "Guru Yoga—A Buddhist Meditative Visualization: Observations Based upon Psychoanalytic Object Relations Theory and Self Psychology." Paper presented to the annual meeting of the American Academy of Religion, Anaheim, Calif.

Bergin, A. E. (1980). "Psychotherapy and Religious Values." *Journal of Consulting and Clinical Psychology,* 48:95–105.

Bernstein, R. (1983). *Beyond Objectivism and Relativism*. Philadelphia: University of Pennsylvania Press.

Blanck, G., and Blanck, R. (1979). *Ego Psychology II*. New York: Columbia University Press.

Bollas, C. (1989). *Forces of Destiny*. London: Free Association Press.

———. (1987). *The Shadow of the Object*. New York: Columbia University Press.

Brenner, C. (1955). *An Elementary Textbook of Psychoanalysis*. Garden City, N.Y.: Doubleday.

Breuer, J., and Freud, S. (1893–1895). *Studies in Hysteria*. In *The Standard Edition of the Complete Psychological Works of Sigmund Freud*. Ed. and trans. James Strachey. London: Hogarth Press, 2:1–305.

Browning, D. (1988). *Religious Thought and the Modern Psychologies*. Minneapolis: Fortress Press.

Buber, M. (1970). *I and Thou*. Trans. W. Kaufmann. New York: Scribner's.

———. (1952). *The Eclipse of God*. New York: Harper and Row.

Chodorow, N. (1989). *Feminism and Psychoanalytic Theory*. New Haven: Yale University Press.

Cuddihy, J. (1974). *The Ordeal of Civility*. New York: Basic Books.

Eissler, K. R. (1958). "Remarks on Some Variations in Psychoanalytical Technique." *International Journal of Psychoanalysis,* 39:222–229.

Erikson, E. (1968). *Identity: Youth and Crisis*. New York: Norton.

Fairbairn, W. R. D. (1943). "The Repression and the Return of Bad Objects." In *An Object Relations Theory of Personality*. New York: Basic Books, 1952.

Fenichel, O. (1941). *Problems of Psychoanalytic Technique*. Albany: Psychoanalytic Quarterly Press.

Fingarette, H. (1963). *The Self in Transformation*. New York: Basic Books.

Flax, J. (1990). *Thinking Fragments: Psychoanalysis, Feminism, and Postmodernism in the Contemporary West*. Berkeley and Los Angeles: University of California Press.

Framo, J. (1970). "Symptoms from a Family Transactional Viewpoint." In N. Ackerman, ed., *Family Therapy in Transition*. Boston: Little, Brown.

Freud, S. ([1940] 1948). *An Outline of Psychoanalysis*. New York: Norton.

———. ([1930] 1962). *Civilization and Its Discontents*. New York: Norton.

———. ([1927] 1964). *The Future of an Illusion*. New York: Doubleday, Anchor.

———. ([1921] 1960). *Group Psychology and the Analysis of the Ego*. New York: Norton.

———. ([1920] 1959). *Beyond the Pleasure Principle*. New York: Bantam.

———. (1914). "Some Reflections on Schoolboy Psychology." In *The Standard Edition of the Complete Psychological Works of Sigmund Freud*. Vol. 13. Ed. and trans. James Strachey. London: Hogarth Press.

———. ([1913] 1952). *Totem and Taboo*. New York: Norton.

Gay, V. (1989). *Understanding the Occult*. Minneapolis: Fortress Press.

Gerhart, M., and Russell, A. (1984). *Metaphoric Process*. Fort Worth: Texas Christian University Press.

Gill, M. (1979). "The Analysis of the Transference." *Journal of the American Psychoanalytic Association*, 263–288.

Greenacre, P. (1959). "Certain Technical Problems in the Transference Relationship." *Journal of the American Psychoanalytic Association*, 7:484–502.

———. (1954). "The Role of Transference." *Journal of the American Psychoanalytic Association*, 2:671–684.

Greenberg, J., and Mitchell, S. (1983). *Object Relations in Psychoanalytic Theory*. Cambridge: Harvard University Press.

Greenson, R. (1967). *The Technique and Practice of Psychoanalysis*. Vol. 1. New York: International Universities Press.

Harlow, H., and Harlow, M. (1969). "Effects of Various Mother-Infant Relations of Rhesus Monkey Behaviors." In B. Foss, ed., *Determinants of Infant Behavior*. Vol. 4. London: Methuen.

Hartmann, H. (1960). *Psychoanalysis and Moral Values*. New York: International Universities Press.

———. (1958). *Ego Psychology and the Problem of Adaption*. New York: International Universities Press.

Hoffman, L. (1981). *Foundations of Family Therapy.* New York: Basic Books.

Homans, P. (1979). *Jung in Context: Modernity and the Making of a Psychology.* Chicago: University of Chicago Press.

———. (1970). *Theology after Freud: An Interpretive Inquiry.* New York: Irvington Press.

Jones, J. (1986). "Macrocosm to Microcosm: Towards a Systemic Theory of Personality." *Journal of Religion and Health,* 25:278–290.

———. (1984). *The Redemption of Matter: Towards the Rapprochement of Science and Religion.* Lanham, Md.: University Press of America.

———. (1982). "The Delicate Dialectic: Religion and Psychology in the Modern World." *Cross Currents,* 32:143–153.

———. (1981). *The Texture of Knowledge: An Essay on Religion and Science.* Lanham, Md.: University Press of America.

———. (1977). "The Lure of Fellowship." *Cross Currents,* 26:420–423.

———. (1972). "Reflections on the Problem of Religious Experience." *Journal of the American Academy of Religion,* 40:445–453.

Jung, K. (1961). *Memories, Dreams and Reflections.* New York: Random House.

———. (1938). *Psychology and Religion.* New Haven: Yale University Press.

Kierkegaard, S. (1941). *Fear and Trembling* and *Sickness unto Death.* Trans. W. Lowrie. Princeton: Princeton University Press.

Kohlberg, L. (1981). *The Philosophy of Moral Development.* New York: Harper and Row.

Kohut, H. (1984). *How Does Analysis Cure?* Chicago: University of Chicago Press.

———. (1977). *The Restoration of the Self.* New York: International Universities Press.

———. (1971). *The Analysis of the Self.* New York: International Universities Press.

Lacan, J. (1978). *Four Fundamental Concepts of Psychoanalysis.* New York: Norton.

Leavy, S. (1988). *In the Image of God.* New Haven: Yale University Press.

———. (1986). "A Pascalian Meditation on Psychoanalysis and Religious Experience." *Cross Currents,* 26:147–155.

———. (1980). *Psychoanalytic Dialogue.* New Haven: Yale University Press.

Loewald, H. (1988). *Sublimation.* New Haven: Yale University Press.

———. (1980). *Papers on Psychoanalysis.* New Haven: Yale University Press.

———. (1978). *Psychoanalysis and the History of the Individual.* New Haven: Yale University Press.

Masterson, J. (1985). *The Real Self.* New York: Brunner Mazel.

McDargh, J. (1988). "Beyond God as Transitional Object." Paper presented to a meeting of the College Theology Society, Los Angeles, Calif.

————. (1983). *Psychoanalytic Object Relations Theory and the Study of Religion*. Lanham, Md.: University Press of America.

Meissner, W. W. (1984). *Psychoanalysis and Religious Experience*. New Haven: Yale University Press.

Messer, S., Sass, L., and Woolfolk, R. (1988). *Hermeneutics and Psychological Theory*. New Brunswick, N.J.: Rutgers University Press.

Mitchell, S. (1988). *Relational Concepts in Psychoanalysis*. Cambridge: Harvard University Press.

Otto, R. (1958). *The Idea of the Holy*. Trans. J. W. Harvey. New York: Oxford University Press.

Phillips, A. (1988). *Winnicott*. Cambridge: Harvard University Press.

Polanyi, M. (1974). *Personal Knowledge*. New York: Harper and Row.

Proudfoot, W. (1985). *Religious Experience*. Berkeley and Los Angeles: University of California Press.

Pruyser, P. (1968). *A Dynamic Psychology of Religion*. New York: Harper and Row.

Racker, H. (1954). "Notes on the Theory of Transference." *Psychoanalytic Quarterly*, 23:78–86.

Rainey, R. (1975). *Freud as a Student of Religion*. AAR Dissertation Series no. 7. Missoula, Mont.: Scholars Press.

Rieff, P. (1959). *Freud: The Mind of the Moralist*. New York: Viking Press.

Rizzuto, A. M. (1979). *The Birth of the Living God*. Chicago: University of Chicago Press.

Robert, M. (1976). *From Oedipus to Moses: Freud's Jewish Identity*. Trans. R. Manheim. Garden City, N.Y.: Doubleday, Anchor.

Roland, A. (1981). "Induced Emotional Reactions and Attitudes in the Psychoanalyst as Transference in Actuality." *Psychoanalytic Review*, 68:45–73.

Schafer, R. (1976). *A New Language for Psychoanalysis*. New Haven: Yale University Press.

Smith, R. S. (1985). "The Becoming of the Person in Martin Buber's Religious Philosophical Anthropology and Heinz Kohut's Psychology of the Self." Ph.D. diss., University of Chicago.

Spence, D. (1982). *Narrative and Historical Truth*. New York: Norton.

Spilka, B., et al. (1975). "Parents, Self and God: A Test of Competing Theories." *Review of Religious Research*, 16:154–165.

————. (1964). "The Concept of God: A Factor-analytic Approach." *Review of Religious Research*, 6:20–35.

Spitz, R. (1946). "Anaclitic Depression." *Psychoanalytic Study of the Child*, 2:313–342.

———. (1945). "Hospitalism." *Psychoanalytic Study of the Child*, 1:53–73.

Stern, D. N. (1985). *The Interpersonal World of the Infant*. New York: Basic Books.

Stolorow, R., and Atwood, G. (1984). "Psychoanalytic Phenomenology: Toward a Science of Human Experience." *Psychoanalytic Inquiry*, 4:87–105.

———. (1979). *Faces in a Cloud: Subjectivity in Personality Theory*. New York: Jason Aronson.

Stolorow, R., Brandchaft, B., and Atwood, G. (1987). *Psychoanalytic Treatment: An Intersubjective Approach*. New York: Analytic Press.

———. (1985). Untitled. Paper presented to the eighth annual conference on self psychology, New York.

———. (1983). "Intersubjectivity in Psychoanalytic Treatment." *Bulletin of the Menninger Clinic*, 47:117–128.

Stolorow, R., and Lachmann, F. (1985). "Transference: The Future of an Illusion." In *The Annual of Psychoanalysis*. Vols. 12–13. New York: International Universities Press.

———. (1980). *Psychoanalysis of Developmental Arrests*. New York: International Universities Press.

Tillich, P. (1966). *On the Boundary*. New York: Scribner's.

———. (1957). *The Dynamics of Faith*. New York: Harper and Row.

———. (1955). *The New Being*. New York: Scribner's.

———. (1952). *The Courage to Be*. New Haven: Yale University Press.

———. (1951). *Systematic Theology*. Vol. 1. Chicago: University of Chicago Press.

———. (1948). *The Shaking of the Foundations*. New York: Scribner's.

Van Herik, J. (1982). *Freud on Femininity and Faith*. Berkeley and Los Angeles: University of California Press.

Vergote, A., and Aubert, C. (1972). "Parental Images and Representations of God." *Social Compass*, 19:431–444.

Vergote, A., et al. (1969). "The Concept of God and Parental Images." *Journal of the Scientific Study of Religion*, 8:79–87.

Winnicott, D. W. (1971). *Playing and Reality*. New York: Routledge.

———. (1965). *The Maturational Process and the Facilitating Environment*. London: Hogarth. (Especially pp. 140–152, "Ego Distortion in Terms of True and False Self" [1960].)

# INDEX

Alexander, Franz, 13
Allport, Gordon, 38
Atwood, George, 24–28
Autonomy and dependency, 17, 20,
  32–33, 91–92, 94–99, 134–
  135. *See also* Self, relational
  model of

"Barbara," case of, 73–76, 132
Bollas, Christopher, 88, 116–125,
  131–134
Buber, Martin, 127–130, 130–134

Culture, theories of, 5–6, 57–61

Defensive self representations, 88–
  91, 100–103, 104–107

Eissler, Kurt, 12
Erikson, Erik, 37, 82, 90–91

Fairbairn, W. R. D., 13–16, 17,
  20–21, 29, 47, 82–83, 105
Faith, psychological nature of, 39–
  40
Feminist theory, 33
Fenichel, Otto, 12
Framo, James, 25–29
Freud, Sigmund: theory of religion,
  1–3, 34–35, 36–38, 51–54, 62,
  64, 81, 99, 111, 112; theory of

culture, 5–6; understanding of
  transference, 9–11, 13, 25–26,
  28; differences from Kohut, 16,
  18–19; relation to Newtonian
  science, 22–24, 48

Gay, Volney, 66
Gill, Merton, 22–24, 27, 110, 112
God representation, 40–41, 42–
  47, 70–76, 80–85, 100–108,
  130–135
Greenacre, Phyllis, 12
Greenson, Ralph, 11–13

"Harold," case of, 69–71, 100–
  104
Hartmann, Heinz, 35, 37

Jung, Carl, 3–5, 25, 36, 47

Kierkegaard, Søren, 123–124, 134
Klein, Melanie, 15, 29
Kohlberg, Lawrence, 81
Kohut, Heinz: differences with
  Freud, 16, 18–19; theory of self
  psychology, 16–22, 27, 28, 43,
  88, 119–120; implications for
  religion, 63–64, 131–134; differences with Masterson, 91–92,
  97–99; understanding of transformation, 92–95, 104–108

Lachmann, Frank, 24–28
Leavy, Stanley, 35, 47–50, 62
Loewald, Hans, 50–57, 62, 133–134

McDargh, John, 40
Mahler, Margaret, 87–88, 91–92, 98–99
"Martin," case of, 76–80, 108–110
Masterson, James, 87–92, 95–96, 98–99, 100, 104, 107
Meissner, William, 35–42, 44, 55, 59, 62, 134

Nietzsche, Friedrich, 123

Object relations theory, 13–22, 30–32, 42–43, 47, 65–66, 87–95, 116–121
Otto, Rudolph, 113–116, 121–122, 124–125, 133

Projective identification, 15, 29, 119
Proudfoot, Wayne, 114

Rizzuto, Ana-Maria: on Freud, 36; on God representation, 40, 42–47, 63–65, 75, 81–82, 134; use of Winnicott, 44–46, 59, 62, 120, 134
Roland, Alan, 29–32

Self, relational model of, 17–22, 28–33, 62–67, 84–85, 91–92, 94–99, 130–135
Selfobjects, 17–22, 63–66, 91–92, 92–95, 105–108, 119–120. *See also* Kohut, Heinz
Self psychology. *See* Kohut, Heinz
Stern, Daniel, 92, 96–99, 134
Stolorow, Robert, 24–28
"Sylvia," case of, 71–73, 104–108
Systems theory, 28–29, 32, 63, 112–113

Tillich, Paul, 125–127, 130–134
Transitional objects. *See* Winnicott, D. W.

Winnicott, D. W.: use by Meissner, 36, 38–42; use by Rizzuto, 44–46, 50; theory of transitional phenomena, 44–46, 57–61, 112, 133–134; critiques of, 55–56; idea of false self, 88; use by Bollas, 116, 120